PLAYING CARDS

IN THE VICTORIA AND ALBERT MUSEUM

SUR
C

Le Ciseaux

Lestoq

Le Pinceau

la Lisse

Le Marbre

Habit de Cartier,

A Paris. Chez Chiquet   Rüe St Jacques au Prés des Mathurins   Auec. Priuil. du Roy.

PLAYING CARDS

IN THE
VICTORIA AND ALBERT MUSEUM

Jean Hamilton

129

LONDON
HER MAJESTY'S STATIONERY OFFICE

© Crown copyright 1988
First published 1988

ISBN 0 11 290461 0

Design by HMSO / Joe Burns

Frontispiece

A 17th century French engraving by
Nicolas de Larmessin, from the V & A collection

CONTENTS

INTRODUCTION

The Victoria and Albert Museum's small but select collection of playing cards has been acquired over the years since the museum's earliest days. Some of the cards have been bought, but most are the gifts of members of the public and other institutions. The collection continues to grow with examples of modern packs, and contains unique material such as designs by D G Rossetti, C F A Voysey and W S Coleman, as well as printing blocks, duty wrappers and other peripheral items. The history of playing cards has been discussed in so many works that rather than giving a complete summary, this short introduction is intended to place the V&A's cards in the context of the periods and countries in which they were produced. Similarly, the origins of the suit signs is a subject in itself, and it is enough here to describe some of the native suits of the European countries whose cards are represented in the collection.

The suit signs of the Germanic packs are acorns, hearts, leaves and bells; the Swiss replace the hearts with shields and the leaves with roses. The French have coeurs, picques, carreaux and trèfles, and from these are derived the English (and American) hearts, spades, diamonds and clubs. The Italian and Spanish suits are cups, swords, money and batons. Variations and hybrids are found in the museum's collection and in others.

The collection contains several examples of tarot cards. The tarot pack consists of 78 cards, but variants of the tarot, such as tarocchino (62 cards) and minichiate (97 cards) are also found. The origin of the symbolic picture cards of the tarot is unknown, though it has been guessed at by various writers on the subject, including Count de Grebelin, who in 1781 suggested that the 22 atutti (picture cards) were derived from the mysteries of the ancient Egyptian religion. Other theories concerning the origins of the personages and scenes on the atutti include an identification of the Emperor with Charlemagne, the woman Pope with the mythical Pope Joan, and the Hanging Man, who is sometimes depicted clutching money bags, with Judas Iscariot. A comprehensive book on the history of the pack is Michael Dummett's *The Game of Tarot*[1], but for an account of the spiritual and divinatory significance of the 'game', the reader is referred to Tom Clarkson's *Tarot the Life Enhancer*[2]. This small but excellent book does much to explain the mystical power of religious symbolism and distilled understanding of the psyche which is inherent in the *atutti*.

The museum's earliest examples of tarot cards are four cards from a late 15th century Italian pack: Stella, the Knave of Money, Death and the Ace of Cups (203)*. These cards were formerly attributed to Antonio di Cicognara because of the resemblance of the design of the Knave of Money to a corresponding card in a pack thought to be by him, which was made for the Visconti-Sforza family in Milan, c1450–53. The Visconti-Sforza pack (74 cards from the set of 78) is divided between the Pierpont Morgan Library in New York, the Accademia Carrara in Bergamo and the private collection of the Colleoni family in Bergamo. The six cards in the Pierpont Morgan Library have been tentatively ascribed to Francesco Zavattari by the Bibliothèque Nationale, Paris, who consider that the Knave of Money is a copy, but Dummett is of the opinion that 'it could well be by (Bonofacio) Bembo', and that the Stella may also resemble a card by Bembo which is now lost. Death and the Ace of Cups do not resemble in any way the Visconti-Sforza pack. The Ace of Cups, with the

---

*Numbers in brackets refer to entries in the 'Designers and Publishers' section – see page 39.

heraldic motto of Isabella d'Este and the Colleoni arms could, according to Dummett, have been painted for Bartolomeo Colleoni (1400–76), but Isabella d'Este, Marchioness of Mantua, 'seems a more likely recipient'.

An example of minichiate is the Florentine pack engraved in the late 18th century, with backs with the Medici arms (207). A non-standard example is the pack also produced in Florence, in 1725, where the cards are lettered with descriptions of historical, biblical and mythical events (204). The cards by Carlo Dellarocca, published c1840 by Gumppenberg in Milan are, according to the Bibliothèque Nationale, an example of the romantic interpretation of the 'Tarot de Marseilles' popular at this period (40). Tarots of the French type appeared in Italy at the beginning of the 18th century. The Italian-produced packs in the collection conclude in date with those published in 1932 by Alessandro Viassone, a Turin firm founded in 1830 (153). A pack of the Marseilles type, probably dating to the mid 18th century, with Italian suit signs and lettered with titles in French, has a back pattern similar to some published by Nicolas François Laudier of Strasbourg, designed by Pierre Isnard in about 1746 (182).

A type of pack known as 'animal' tarot originated in Bavaria; the numerals of these cards have animal subjects, usually with the exception of the first and last cards, which are a harlequin and a musician, or a harlequin and a juggler. A set of 38 animal tarots in the collection, published c1770 in Munich, has as the last card a man balancing a hat on a stick on his nose (199). Another of the same genre, published by P Bruck of Luxembourg in the late 18th century, is unfortunately incomplete, consisting of only 21 cards (19); a complete pack by this maker is in the British Museum's Schreiber Collection (O'Donoghue, No 130)[3]. Another version of tarot, published by Dondorf of Frankfurt in 1887, has the court cards representing famous people and the Aces famous European buildings (41); a similar pack with views of Copenhagen and its environs was issued by Holmblads of Copenhagen, c1865 (91). A Viennese version, designed by J Neumayer and produced by Piatnik in the late 19th century, is one of a series of only

54-card packs known as *Industrie und Gluck* (Industry and Fortune), the numerals double-ended and with various oriental and rural imaginary scenes (127). Another of the packs of the same period, with French suit signs, is by J Nejedly of Vienna (126).

Of the French packs in the collection, Lequart's *Tarot Allemagne*, published in the 1890s, is an unusual set – double-ended, with French suits and numerals with chinoiserie scenes (113). Two packs by B P Grimaud, successor to the ancient firm of Arnoult, were issued in the last quarter of the 19th century; both have Italian suit signs. One, however, is double-ended and a Marseilles pattern (75); the other has full-length figures, and the numerals II and V are lettered *Junon* and *Jupiter* respectively (76). J Muller & Cie of Schaffhausen and Hasle, from 1889–1940, is represented in the collection with a traditional Marseilles pack, published c1914 (122). A unique set is the pack of 24 cards entitled *Bilder zum Tarot* (tarot pictures), an interpretation of the Major Arcana – like the *atutti*, the picture cards of the tarot – published in 1984 by the designer, Helmut Wonschick of Berlin (163). As a form of playing card the tarot was never popular in England, but the collection contains the pack of cartomantic cards designed by Pamela Colman Smith and published by A E Waite in 1916 (146); similar sets have been published in America in this century.

Yet another form of the tarot, used for fortune-telling, are the 'etteilla'. These were the invention of a French wigmaker named Alliette, who was inspired by Count de Grebelin's theories of mystical symbolism. The etteilla (Alliette spelt backwards) is composed of the traditional 78 cards, but some of the personages of the Major Arcana appear with different titles – thus 'Le Pendu' becomes 'La Prudence', 'L'Amoureux' becomes 'Mariage' and 'La Maison Dieu' becomes 'Misere' or 'Prison', and so on. One etteilla, published by the widow Gueffier (Paris 1807) entitled *Le Petit Oracle des Dames*, is a 42-card pack, etched and colour-stencilled, and with miniature cards carrying the suit signs within the designs (81A).

Among the oldest cards in the collection are five in the style of Clas Oth, printed in the early or mid

16th century (129). These, formerly in the possession of Major Henry Harvard, consist of a Knave of Acorns, a Knave of Bells, a Five of Acorns, a Four of Leaves and an Eight of Leaves. They are of the same type as the cards which were discovered in the binding of a 15th century book and exhibited by Dr Stukely at the Society of Antiquaries in 1763 (Willshire, G 1)[4]. They are probably from Nuremberg and may be dated between 1546 and 1550, but the Deuce of Acorns in the 'Stukely' pack has the device of a unicorn and shield with crossed hammers, whereas in packs by Clas Oth dating between 1540 and 1555, the Deuce of Acorns shows a seated lion and a scroll with his name. The crossed hammers are a device used in the shields of cities in the mining areas of eastern Germany.

A single card, the Nine of Rabbits or Hares (131), is circular and engraved, from a set published c1470 now thought to be the work of the 'Master P W of Cologne', with suit signs of animals and flowers. Also engraved are the Five of Monkies, the Five of Peacocks and the One of Parrots from a 52-card pack by Virgil Solis, probably issued in about 1544 (148). Other engraved cards are the set of 47 copies by W Y Ottley (130), published by him in *A Collection of Fac-Similes of Scarce and Curious Prints* (London 1828). The originals are 15th century cards which have been attributed variously to Israel van Maecken, Martin Schoengauer, the monogrammist MZ, or alternatively to Nikolaus Mair of Landshut. A set of 36 cards (82), printed from unique engraved silver plates in the collection of Friedrich von Rothenburg and issued in 1881 by Dr K Förster, was attributed by Förster to Georg Heinrich Bleich. The monogram *HGB F* is on the Six of Leaves, but according to Thieme & Becke's dictionary, it cannot be attributed to Bleich, and is suggested to be that of Heinrich Godig or Goedig (1531–1606), of Brunswick. The cards depict animals playing musical instruments, the King of Bells is a throned Ethiopian, the Queen is a standing figure in early 16th century costume, the Six of Hearts is a bird, and so on.

The collection contains several sheets of cards. One of these, formerly belonging to Major Henry Harvard, has six cards, the knaves of hearts and diamonds, and is, according to Séguin, probably of late 15th century Lyonnais workmanship (142). On the Knave of Diamonds are the initials G S (perhaps Giles Savouré). Another sheet, a modern impression, is from a block possibly produced by Jean Goyrand of Lyons in the late 15th century, or by Jehan Volay, also of Lyons, who worked in the 16th century (156). Two sheets of eight cards each, four kings and four queens, were produced in Rouen or Lyons in the early 16th century (47); one is signed with the initial F on *grants baslive*. A woodblock for printing a sheet of 36 standard south German cards, and – from the reverse of the block – 10 cards (five knaves and five kings), bearing the name Fetscher and the initial F on the knaves, was probably produced in Munich in the late 18th century (48). A Josef Fetscher of Burggasse, Munich, was working in the early 19th century. A sheet for a Swiss pack of 42 cards published at Basle, c1500, is illustrated by Schreiber (230). Another modern impression, from a Spanish block made in the 18th century, may be by Felix Solesio & Sons of Madrid (147). There is also a Lippmann reproduction of a sheet of 16 cards from a pack supposedly by H S Beham (235), but this attribution is denied by Pauli[5].

A late 17th century pack of hombre cards is of Spanish type – the Knight takes the place of the Queen and the coat of arms on the Ace of Money is possibly that of Ferdinand and Isabella, but the inscriptions are in Italian, and it is possibly a Sicilian pack, published by Antonino Monasta (118). Other late 17th century examples include a Deuce of Shields and a Knave of Shields, from a Swiss pack with backs decorated with the cross and octagon pattern also found on German cards dating to the 16th century (231). One card, the Ace of Acorns, depicting the Constellation of the Raven, is from a pack by Philip Harsdörfer of Nuremburg (87). Harsdörfer published what was probably the first pack of astronomical cards in 1656, and reissues appeared in 1663, 1668 and 1674. Another non-standard pack, depicting the coats of arms of sovereigns, states, princes and nobles of Europe, was published by Claude Orance Finé (called De Brianville) at Lyons, c1658 (49). The set (which is lacking five cards) is decorated on the backs with a German cross and hexagon pattern. An English version of these heraldic cards, forming a manual of heraldry and dedicated to the Duke of Albemarle, was published by Richard Blome, c1677 (17).

Among the most interesting of the English packs of this period are the politico-historical playing cards dealing with the Titus Oates conspiracy, known as 'The Popish Plot' (7). By an unidentified engraver (possibly James Kirkall), they are based on pencil designs by Francis Barlow, one of the earliest English illustrators. There are variations of this pack: one advertised by Robert Walton 'at the Globe on the north side of St Paul's Churchyard', on 26 December 1679, is possibly the second of the series. Thirty-six cards (from a pack of 52) have the same back pattern as the Popish Plot pack, and depict incidents in the defeat of the Spanish Armada (167). According to Sylvia Mann[6], a later edition of this pack was published by John Lenthall in the early 18th century under the title *Navigational Cards*. Another politico-historical set, *Marlborough's Victories*, was published c1708 (170).

A pack published by Lenthall, c1710 and sold 'at Willerton's Toy Shop, Bond Street', entitled *Love Cards, or The Intrigues and Amusements of that Passion merrily display'd* (111) is probably a later edition of his *Delightful Cards*, published c1660–62 (Guildhall Collection, No 544)[7]. Another pack with the inscription of Willerton's Toy Shop is an educational set, with the rulers of England on the court cards and the numerals of each suit with multiplication and other tables (172). It is no earlier than 1760, but could also be by Lenthall or his successors. The pack known as 'The Rump Parliament', of which only three complete sets exist, was probably made in Holland during Charles II's exile, and is represented in the collection by a lithographed reproduction, published by Edmund Goldschmid in 1886 (234). Other 'educational' packs include a set of biblical cards illustrating episodes from the Old Testament, finely etched by Antonio Visentini in 1748 after designs by Francesco Zuccarelli (155), and *The Elements of Astronomy and Geography Explained on 40 Cards*, engraved and coloured by the Abbé Paris

and published by John Wallis in 1795 (133).

An early 18th century pack of 36 cards produced by J C Weigel of Augsburg depicts the costumes of Augsburg (162); some of the images are derived from a series of 21 costume plates published by Jeremias Wolff in 1720. A similar pack, also published by Weigel, is in the Museum of Playing Cards at Frankfurt, and others are described by O'Donoghue in his catalogue of the Schreiber Collection at the British Museum[8]. A small collection of 19th century impressions of standard mid 18th century southern German packs, which include some published by Jacob Frankenberger (53) and some by Joseph Hensler, were the gift of the Bavarian National Museum in 1885 (90), and some later 18th century cards by the Backofens (Johann Ernst, Johann Mattias and Wilhelm) were acquired in 1910 (3,4). In the same gift was an anonymous pack of 'geographical' cards describing the divisions of Bavaria (200), and a single card (201), the Würst (sausage), from a pack of 32 for the game known as Hexespiel (Witches Game) or Vogelspiel (Bird Game). This game originated in Italy where it was called Cuccu (Cuckoo). Two oddities in the collection, which appear to be unique, are a woven silk pack with the name Panichi and what may be the weaver's mark, presumably made in Italy in the late 18th or early 19th century (132), and one French 18th century 'card', the *Pallas*, of coloured and inlaid mother-of-pearl (181).

Transformation cards, a phenomenon that first appeared in the early 19th century, are divided into printed and published packs, ordinary standard cards which have been turned into transformations by amateur artists, and completely homemade packs. Basically they consist of drawings which — as the name suggests — transform the suit signs into comic illustrations. The earliest and most distinguished of the printed sets are those published by J G Cotta of Tübingen, and the first of these is in the collection (105), published in 1805 after designs by the Countess Jennison-Walworth; the court cards illustrate characters in Schiller's play *Die Jungfrau von Orleans* (1802). The Cotta packs were issued in almanacs, between 1805 and 1811. An engraved pack by H F Müller of Vienna is in the same vein (119). A copy of Müller's pack, which was published in Ackermann's *Repository of Arts* (London 1818–19) is also in the collection (120). A lithographed transformation piquet pack published in Paris in 1873 has animal-headed figures on the court cards of the hearts and diamonds suits (188). An English printed pack by 'Crowquill' (Alfred Forrester) was published by Reynolds & Sons, c1845 (26), and another lithographed set of about twenty years later was issued by Maclure, Macdonald and Macgregor of Manchester (116).

Five designs for a pack which was never published, by the Pre-Raphaelite painter Dante Gabriel Rossetti, contain caricatures of Louis Philippe as King of Diamonds, Mr Punch as King of Clubs, and Queen Victoria as Queen of Hearts (140). In the politico-historical tradition E T Reed, Punch cartoonist, designed a deck entitled *Panko or Votes for Women*. This pack, a variant of the game of Snap, depicts the political figures, opponents and supporters of the suffragette movement (136). Of the European packs, *Jeep* has aces with caricatures of the second world war English, American, French and Russian leaders, with Adolf Hitler as the Joker. This was published by Leonard Biermans SA, in Belgium, c1943–44 (9). A traditional Snap game was issued by John Jacques & Son in 1885 (104); five cards from this pack are incorporated in Peter Blake's 'Snap II', which is in the V&A's Department of Paintings (11).

W S Coleman, better known for his drawings of 19th century nymphettes, which appeared on numerous greetings cards, and for his ceramic designs, is represented by a design in the Japanese style for the backs of an unidentified pack (23). The famous flat-pattern designer C F A Voysey also designed the backs of an unpublished deck (157). Some luxury cards were produced by De La Rue & Co. The backs of one pack have a pattern of lilies and violets surrounding a shield of pretence (106), and may possibly be the work of Owen Jones, who produced 173 designs for De La Rue between 1844 and 1864. Another of this firm's packs was published to celebrate the Great Exhibition of 1851, with the coats of arms of Victoria and Albert embossed in gold on the backs (29). Sir

Henry Cole stated in his autobiography that his last attempt in 'Art Manufactures' was the production in 1874 of international playing cards, designed by Reuben Townroe and published by De La Rue. This pack shows European Royalties, the presidents of the United States and Switzerland and John Brown, Queen Victoria's servant (149). The cards belonging to the V&A have plain red backs, but a pack in the British Museum (Willshire, E 173[9]) is decorated with the royal arms of England and of Saxe-Coburg-Gotha, printed in gold on a blue ground.

Twentieth century English packs in the collection include a Snap game designed, lithographed and screenprinted by the staff and students of the Royal College of Art, c1975 (10), and *The Deck of Cards*, published by Andrew Jones Art in 1979, is also the work of several designers (89). The politico-historical theme is carried through to the present day with the screenprinted pack *Playing Politics or Cabinet Shuffle*, published by the V&A in 1983 (143). The aces and jokers show the Prime Minister, Margaret Thatcher, and members of the four main political parties caricatured by major cartoonists including Gerald Scarfe and Marc Boxer. An accompanying leaflet by Yashna Beresiner and Nicky Bird gives a short history of this genre of playing card and biographies of the artists. The pack designed by A M Cassandre (Adolphe Mouron) is typical of the non-standard cards of postwar France, with lively and original interpretations of the traditional court figures; it was published by Hermès of Paris in 1950 (21).

There is only one example of a Chinese pack – 81 cards from a full set of 105 (168). These are finger-shaped cards: known as 'dominoes' because of the spot numbering of the suits, they also have coins, scrolls and other symbols emblematic of the blessings of life. The only other examples of Far Eastern packs are the five Thai sets (232), used to play the game Pai Tong, and a Japanese pack, *The Poem Game* (210). The former resemble the Chinese cards, but the suits are birds, men and eyes; they were the gift of Colonel Amnuay Chya-Rochana in 1952. There is one deck of Greek cards, published by the 'Hope' company in the late 19th century, at Corfu (202). The group of Russian packs are either

French or German suited, and include the well-known trappola set, the *Circus* (211), and some decorative non-standard cards (225), their double-ended courts with Egyptian, Chinese, African and Russian figures, and the aces a ship, a lion, a leopard and an eagle. The Indian playing cards, which are in the charge of the Indian Department of the museum, have been fully catalogued by Rudolf von Leyden in *Ganjifa, the Playing Cards of India* (Victoria and Albert Museum, London, 1982).

The collection includes a few standard packs which have a secondary purpose as advertising material, printed as special orders for various firms and institutions, with backs decorated with trademarks, badges and so on. There are several standard and non-standard packs produced in England, Holland, Belgium, Germany, Austria, Spain, Denmark, Sweden, Canada and the USA which have not been mentioned in this introduction. All the cards are listed alphabetically in the catalogue under the publishers' or the designers' names. Those which remain unidentified are to be found in the Anonymous section in alphabetical and chronological order under the countries where they were produced. Wherever possible, reference is made to catalogues raisonnées, which are abbreviated in the entries and listed in full at the end, where there is also a bibliography of other works consulted or cited.

JDH

NOTES

1   Michael Dummett, *The Game of Tarot*, (London, 1980)

2   Tom Clarkson, *Tarot the Life Enhancer*, (Woking, 1983)

3   F M O'Donoghue, *Catalogue of the Collection of Playing Cards bequeathed to the Trustees of the British Museum by the late Lady Charlotte Schreiber*, (London, 1901)

4   W H Willshire, *A Descriptive Catalogue of Playing and Other Cards in the British Museum accompanied by a Concise General History of the Subject and Remarks on Cards of Divination and of a Politico – Historical Character*, (London, 1876)

5   G Pauli, *Hans Sebald Beham*, (Strasbourg, 1901)

6   Sylvia Mann, *Collecting Playing Cards*, (Worcester & London, 1966)

7   Guildhall Collection, Guildhall Library and Art Gallery

8   F M O'Donoghue, *op cit*

9   W H Willshire, *op cit*

THE PLATES

178

157

89

ENGLAND

Among the earliest English packs, which date to the late 17th and early 18th centuries, is the politico-historical *Popish Plot* (7), which deals with the Titus Oates conspiracy of 1678. There are variations of this pack, which is based on the pencil drawings of Francis Barlow. Alfred Henry Forrester, whose pseudonym was 'Crow-quill', designed the caricature transformation pack (26) published in 1845 by Reynolds & Sons, London. The fashion for transformation cards dates to the early 19th century, and packs such as the colour lithograph one issued in 1865 by Maclure, Macdonald and Macgregor of Manchester (116) show their continued popularity into the later part of the century. De La Rue & Co produced some luxury cards with a back pattern of lilies and violets surrounding a shield of pretence (106). The design is possibly by Owen Jones, who made 173 designs for De La Rue between 1844 and 1864. Also by

this firm is a pack of cards with figures in period costume, with plain yellow backs (30). Snap, the popular family game, originated in the mid 19th century, and the 1885 pack by John Jacques & Son Ltd, with letterpress captions, is a classic example (104). A non-standard pack with pseudo-French figures (152) was designed by Aymer Vallance, an early writer on William Morris, and published by the Peerless Playing Card Company around the turn of the century. The backs carry a styl-ized flower and leaf design: another design for a back pattern is by C F A Voysey, the architect and flat-pattern designer (157). *The Deck of Cards* by Adrian Heath and other artists (89) was published in 1979 by Andrew Jones Art, London.

The Conspirators Signing ye Resolve for killing ye King.

"Oh, you little monster!"

21   144

FRANCE

The suit signs of French cards are coeurs, picques, carreaux and trèfles, and from these are derived the English and American hearts, spades, diamonds and clubs. Claude Orance Finé (called De Brianville) published the set of heraldic cards (49), depicting sovereigns, states, princes and nobles of Europe, at Lyons c1658, and an English version of these cards, forming a manual of heraldry, was published by Richard Blome in c1677. The hybrid tarot pack of Marseilles pattern, with Italian suit signs and lettered with titles in French (182), is from an unidentified publisher, but the back pattern was designed by Pierre Isnard, c1746. In packs of the Paris pattern the court cards were named after kings, queens, gods and goddesses; this single Pallas of Spades (183) is from a pack dating probably to the third quarter of the 18th century. It has a plain back, and was used as an invitation card. A transformation piquet pack, with animal-headed figures on the court cards of hearts and diamonds (188), was published

in Paris in 1873. Another piquet pack of this period, with a back pattern of bees in gold (117), was published by Charles Maurin & Cie. *Cartes Indiennes* (77), with court cards depicting Indian rulers, was published by B P Grimaud (successor to the mid 19th century firm of Arnoult) around 1900. The Ace of Clubs bears the duty stamp of the Republic (1890). Grimaud also published *Hollandaises Illustrées* (144), a whist pack designed c1910 by F Simon, with figures in 16th century costume and backs with butterflies, and *Jeu Louis XV* (80), a reprint of a 19th century pack, published in 1920. A more recent pack (21), printed from colour half-tone blocks, was designed by Adolphe Mouron (Cassandre) and published by Hermès in 1950. It is typical of non-standard cards of postwar France, with lively and original interpretations of traditional court figures.

16

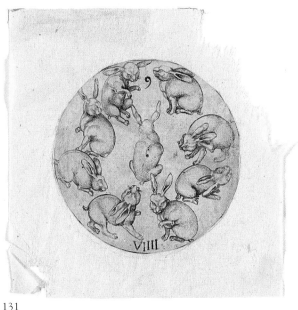

131   82

AUSTRIA and GERMANY

One of the earliest cards in the collection, the Nine of Rabbits or Hares (131) dates to c1470 and is attributed to the 'Master PW of Cologne'. It is from an engraved circular pack in which the suit signs are animals and flowers. Three cards – the One of Parrots, Five of Peacocks and Five of Monkies (148) – are from another decorative pack, engraved with birds and animals, by Virgil Solis, issued c1544. The Six of Leaves (82), printed c1881 from silver plates in Count Friedrich von Rothenburg's possession, carries the monogram *HGB F* – possibly Heinrich Godig of Brunswick, who flourished in the 16th and early 17th centuries. Another 36-card hand-coloured pack depicts the costumes of Augsburg (161): published by J C Weigel, it owes some of its designs to Jeremias Wolff, who issued a set of costume plates in 1720. A set of woodcut cards, published c1810 by J H Crato of Lüneburg, has court cards with full-length figures and the numerals with putti

engaged in various pursuits; the backs are paste paper patterns (24). The Backofen brothers worked in Nuremberg in the late 18th and early 19th centuries: one standard pack by Johann Ernst Backofen (2) has hand-coloured woodcuts with a seaweed pattern on the backs. Joseph Glanz of Vienna published the 36-card pack (60) with court card figures in pseudo-historic costume, and the colour-stencilled piquet pack with chequer-pattern backs (108) came from E Knepper & Co, founded in Vienna c1862. The hand-coloured etched pack for a fortune-telling game, Comisches Lotteriespiel, with motto cards in German and French (81) was designed by Grünewald – possibly Felix Grünewald, who worked in Nuremberg around 1820–40.

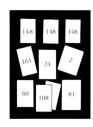

Eine vornehme Jungfrau im Win=
ter mitgehend.
Fille de Condition sortant en Hyver.

E 6308.2 - 1910

6.

Wein zum Trinken in einem See,
Knaster dazu — Teremtete!
Du vin à boire dans un lac et du ca=
nastre — Teremtete!

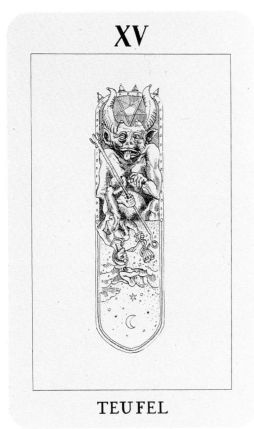

XV

TEUFEL

163

119

AUSTRIA and GERMANY

In Knepper's colour-stencilled trappola pack (109), published c1860, the knaves of each suit depict Swiss heroes and the deuces the four seasons; the backs carry a plaid pattern. Two examples of 19th century miniature packs were published at Frankfurt, one by C L Wüst (167), the other by Dondorf (44). Dondorf's is a Patience pack, with court cards and aces representing the four continents and backs depicting birds round a fountain. The firm of Bernhard J Dondorf was founded in 1833 and closed 100 years later: two other packs in the collection are a tarot pack (41) with famous people on the court cards and buildings of Europe on the aces, and the elaborately pretty fin-de-siècle *Baronesse* whist pack (43). Two late 19th century Viennese packs are Johann Nejedly's etched tarocco pack with zig-zag patterned backs (126), and a tarot pack from a series called Industrie und Gluck (Industry and Fortune), published by Piatnik (127). The pack, designed by J Neumayer, has double-ended numerals depicting rural scenes and figures. A unique set of 24 cards illustrating the Major Arcana of the tarot was published in 1984 by the artist, Helmut Wonschick, in Berlin (163), and Müller's transformation pack (119), issued in the *Repository of Arts*, depicts the Viennese story of 'Beatrice'.

20

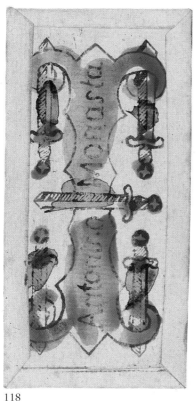

118   203

ITALY

Four court cards from a late 15th century Milanese pack – Stella, the Knave of Money, Death (wearing a Cardinal's hat) and the Ace of Cups – are the museum's earliest examples of tarots (203). Formerly attributed to Antonio di Cicognara, they are handpainted and were probably made for Isabella d'Este, Marchioness of Mantua. Forty cards of the Neapolitan pattern were published, perhaps in Sicily, by Antonino Monasta in the late 17th or early 18th centuries, but the designs are Spanish, with the Queen replaced by a knight (118). Minichiate, a game derived from the tarot, was first heard of in 1415; it has a pack of 96 or 97 cards. *Minichiate Istoriche* (204), published in Florence in 1725, depicts historical events of Persia, Rome, Greece and Assyria. The backs show a figure emblematic of history seated among the ruins of Rome. Another minichiate pack of late 18th century Florentine publication has the arms of the Medici family on the backs (207). Antonio Visentini's etched 'biblical' cards (155) after designs by Francesco Zuccarelli, 1748, have suit signs of discs, diamonds, hearts and jars; each card illustrates an episode from the Old Testament. A unique pack of woven silk cards (132) has the name G I O Panichi on the Six of Hearts. The backs carry engraved figures of 17th century halberdiers holding shields with the Medici arms; the pack is therefore probably Florentine, and dates to the late 18th or early 19th century. Designs by G Boriota for pseudo-historical costume cards were published in 1882 by Luigi Adami of Florence; the backs have a blue marble pattern (13). The Genoese firm of Armanino Fratelli published a pack of standard whist cards with French suits in 1908 (1), and the latest Italian-produced pack in the collection is the pack of 78 Piedmontese tarots, published in 1932 by Alessandro Viassone, Turin (153). Gumppenberg of Milan published c1840 a set of cards engraved by Carlo Dellarocca (40); they are said to be an example of the romantic interpretation of the 'Tarot de Marseilles' popular at this period.

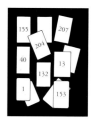

Sapienza da Salom. Ecco la vera Sapi-
Ecclesiastico com- enza divina, ed
posto da Iehu humana, ecco la ve-
Libri Morali, ra morale Filosof.
utilissimi. cont.ᵃ a quella
del Mondo.

Questi Libri Celesti ognun che le
L'umana impara, e la Divina leg.
Humana, ac Divina simul Sapientia splend.
Quam bene in hif librif discite, qui legiti
Due Ale con una Stella sop.ind. Sapienza.

XXXIII

RATTO DELLE SABINE

XXXIIII

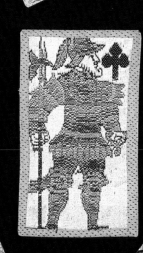

E 822 (40) - 1939

TESTIS TEMPORUM

XI

LA FORZA

E 1866·13 - 1885

GENOVA

27

123

HOLLAND and BELGIUM

Belgian and Dutch cards have the English and French suit signs, and the woodcut cards by J T Dubois, published in the first quarter of the 19th century, have Paris pattern court cards (45). A pack published by Fabrica de Daveluy of Bruges in the third quarter of the 19th century, however, has the numerals as cups, swords, batons and money in the Italian and Spanish style (27). The court cards carry figures of rulers and warriors of Europe, and the backs have a seaweed pattern. A Belgian pack with an unusual Joker and aces with topographical scenes was probably published by Brepols S A of Turnhout (17). The backs have a pattern of dogs' heads with interlinked collar chains. 'Nederland' Speelkaarten-fabriek published a pack with Dutch topographical

scenes on the aces and a red cube pattern on the backs in the second quarter of this century (123). *Hollandia Whist*, another pack of the period by this firm, has court cards with figures in national costume and backs decorated with a Dutch tile pattern (124). In 1943–44 Leonard Biermans S A of Turnhout issued *Jeep* – a whist pack anticipating the liberation of Belgium (9). The aces have caricatures of General Eisenhower, De Gaulle, Stalin and Montgomery; the Joker is a caricature of Adolf Hitler and the backs are decorated with a Jeep.

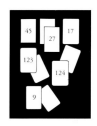

52

SPAIN

There are two cards from unidentified 19th century packs in the collection, the Two of Cups (229), a colour-stencilled woodcut, and the Three of Money (228), which has a large leaf pattern in blue on the back. Vicente Gombau of Madrid published a pack of standard cards in 1856 with a back pattern of tangled blue lines (66): a pack with a similar pattern, but in red, was published by Juan Humanes y Ca in 1865 (94). Two unidentified miniature packs dating c1870 have standard suits and backs with a trellis and star pattern, one in red and one blue (226). The Barcelona firm Fulladosa y Ca published a pack of 48 woodcut and stencilled cards in 1872 with full-length figures representing Europe, Africa, Asia and America on the court cards and backs with a diagonal plaid pattern (54). Another pack of 48,

the backs patterned with blue and pink interlacing, was published by Fabrica De Barajas de Olea of Cadiz in the third quarter of the 19th century (128). The game of ombre, or hombre, is played with a pack of 40 cards, omitting the eight, nine and ten of each suit. Braulio Fournier, of Burgos, published two colour-lithographic hombre packs c1870, both with the tangled blue line pattern on the backs (50,51). Another Fournier, Heraclio, was working at Vitoria, Spain, c1880. The standard pack issued by him has a similar back pattern in brown (52), and was exhibited at the Paris Exhibition of 1878.

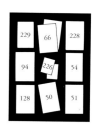

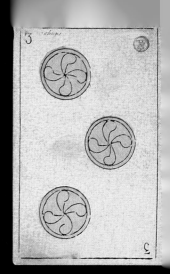

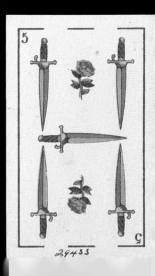

219

225

RUSSIA and GREECE

The Russian packs in the collection were published by the Playing Card Monopoly at St Petersburg in the late 19th century. In 1842 Paul, brother of Thomas De La Rue, was appointed Superintendent of the Monopoly, which was supplied by his brother's London firm with paper and ink. He also imported expertise. All but one of the packs in the collection have French suit signs and nearly all bear the duty stamp of the Foundling Hospital, whose seal was impressed, usually on the Ace of Diamonds, beneath the Russian eagle. The Monopoly's profits were intended to support the hospital. A pack of 36 trappola cards, known as the 'Circus' pack (211), is German suited with circus figures on the suit of leaves, and bears the Foundling Hospital stamp on the Deuce of Bells. In another pack of non-standard cards (219) the King of Hearts holds the suit sign in a drinking vessel, the Knave of Hearts is a Harlequin, the Queen of Clubs

plays a harp and the Knave of Diamonds a trumpet. A third pack (225) has double-ended court cards representing Egyptian, Chinese, African and Russian figures; the aces are a ship, a leopard, a lion and an eagle and the backs have a star trellis pattern. The backs of all the packs are colourful, with trellis, plaid or arabesque patterns, such as on the costume cards with figures in armour or 16th century dress (217). There is only one Greek pack in the collection (202); the cards have Italian suit signs and the court cards show figures of ancient heroes. It was published at Corfu by the 'Hope' playing card makers in the late 19th century. The backs display a classical vase of flowers on a pedestal.

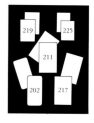

93

CZECHOSLOVAKIA
and other countries

The suit signs of Czechoslovakian cards correspond to the Germanic acorns, hearts, leaves and bells, and all the cards in this collection were published in Prague in the 19th century. A standard late pack with a plaid pattern in black on the backs was published by M Baller or Ballek (5). The Deuce of Acorns bears a duty-paid stamp, a double-headed eagle. A pack of 32 cards of a standard Bohemian pattern, with zig-zag patterned backs, was published c1860 by Antonis Kratochvil (110), successor to M Severy of Prague. The duty stamp 'K K Kartenstempel 30' appears with the maker's name on the Eight of Bells. An early 19th century pack of 32 fortune-telling cards, with titles in German and Czechoslovakian, was published by F Macchi of Prague (115). The collection holds just the numeral cards of a Bavarian 'animal' tarot pack published by Pet. Bruck in Luxem-bourg in the late 19th century; its back patterns are blue and yellow blotch (19). Two Swedish packs of standard cards with the Paris pattern were published by Lithografiska Aktiebolaget, Norrköping, in the third quarter of the 19th century (114); the backs have a diagonal pattern of dots and swirls, one in red and one blue. Danish cards are represented in the collection by two standard packs and two tarot packs published by L P Holmblads Fabrik in Copenhagen between 1860 and 1865. The standard packs (91) have backs patterned with dotted flowers on diagonal stems, and the tarots (93) have French suit signs and views on the numerals.

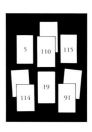

v PRAZE

CESAR

CESAR

IX

X

140   140

EDUCATIONAL
and others

One of the collection's 'educational' packs depicts the rulers of England on the hearts, diamonds and clubs suits, and the numerals are printed with multiplication and measurement tables (172). This pack, dated c1760–70 was sold at Willerton's Toy Shop. Richard Blome's heraldic cards (12), c1677, also come into the educational category, as do the 39 cards (39) from a pack of historical subjects after Stefano Della Bella, published in an unidentified German edition of the late 17th or early 18th centuries. Another 'educational' pack of 63 cards, John Jacques' *The Counties of England*, shows the chief towns and industries of England in the third quarter of the 19th century (102). The 'Perseverance' series by Goodall is an example of an early 20th century standard pack, with a decorative pattern of vine leaves on the backs (70). The back pattern of another Goodall pack, c1898, has a design composed of bicycle parts, reflecting the craze for cycling among young men and women of the 1890s (69). W S Coleman's design for a back pattern is a fairly early example of the Anglo-Japanese style (23), and unique in the collection are the five designs for an unpublished pack by the eminent Pre-Raphaelite painter Rossetti, which include caricatures of Queen Victoria and Louis Philippe (140). The Great Mogul wrapper (97) is included with a pack by Hunt & Sons, c1810; this motif was first used by Philip Blanchard in the 18th century. Henry Hart's pack bears a portrait of Henry VIII (88); Hart, of Red Lion Street, Holborn was probably a son of the Henry Hart who was Master of the Worshipful Company of Makers of Playing Cards, 1763–64. The 1803 engraved example of a duty stamp (18), the Ace of Spades, is by Brotherton, an unknown maker.

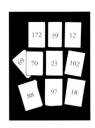

ANN

began her Reign
March.8.:1702 | Reign'd
12Y:4 M:&23D:

Der ♥ König.

Nimrod

der erste Monarch, wird ein stär=
cker Jäger für Gott genañt, wel=
chet erstlich den wilden Thiern
nachgehends auch den Menschē
nachgestellt, und sie zu seine dien=
sten bezwungen. Hat regieret
nach erschaffung der Welte
ungefehr 1700.

Beasts four
footed Ani=
=mals

(1) G. a Elephant passant A. (2) er. a Bull passant
G. (3) A. on a mount q.y. a stagg lodged G. (4) A.
a stagg tripping q.g. attired O. (5) er. a stagg sprin=
=ging forward O. (6) A. a Unicorn seiant S. armed
O. (7) A. a Bear rampant S. mussled O. (8) B. a wolfe
saliant A. (9) er. a grey hound currant A. collored
O. (10) A. 3 corner S. (11) A. 3 a a mountaines in pale
passant S. (12) A. a chevron B. between 3 squirills
seiant G.

9.
NOTTINGHAM.

Robin Hood in the Forest of Sherwood.
He was famous from 1189 to 1247.
Manufactory of Stockings and Lace.
POPULATION, 58,000.

GREAT MOGUL

Succrs. to Mattw. Gibson.
HUNT & SON,
Card Makers to his MAJESTY.
53. Mortimer Street London.

G.III. REX.
HONISOIT QUI MALY PENSE
No 14
DIRUET MON DROIT

EXPORTATION
BROTHERTON

1803

210

210

FACSIMILES and others

Certain rare packs have been reproduced in facsimile, including *A Pack of Cavalier Playing Cards* (233), and *The Rump Parliament*, or *A complete political satire of the Commonwealth* (234), both published by Edmund Goldschmid for the Aungervyle and Clarendon Historical Societies in Edinburgh, 1885–86. A Lippmann reproduction (235) of a sheet of 16 cards attributed to Hans Sebald Beham (1500–50) was acquired in 1934. William Young Ottley's *A Collection of Fac-Similes of Scarce and Curious Prints* etc, of 1828, includes 47 cards from a pack of 52 with Italian suits and with the money suits represented by pomegranates (130). It is variously attributed to several artists including Nikolaus Mair, Israel van Maecken and Martin Schoengauer. A single card depicting the Constellation of the Raven (87), produced by Philip Harsdörfer of Nuremberg in the late 17th century, is from probably the first astronomical pack, issued by Harsdörfer in 1656, and reissued in 1663 and 1674. Between 1774 and 1776 Rowley & Co attempted to change the traditional suit signs in a pack with portraits of the kings and queens of England, France, Spain and Russia, and cups, clover leaves, diamonds and spearheads replacing the hearts, diamonds, spades and clubs (141). This attempt, which produced a pretty pack, did not succeed in becoming popular. A Japanese pack, *The Poem Game*, consists of figure cards and cards inscribed with poems (210), and an oddity in the collection is a French card of indeterminate date made of mother-of-pearl (181). John Lenthall's *Love Cards, or The Intrigues and Amusements of that Passion merrily display'd*, published c1710, contains a caricature of Sir John Hewson, the regicide, on the Ace of Hearts (111). Hewson also appears in a pack entitled *Delightful Cards* (see 112, not illustrated), issued by Lenthall c1660–62, in the Guildhall Collection.

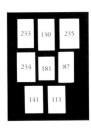

X ♣

O liver seeking God while the K. is murthered by his order.

VI

IsP

IIII ♥

The Rump roasted salt it well it stinks exceedingly.

DAVID

♠

Das Aß.

Der Raab.

Dieses Gestirn hat 7. Sterne/ deren 4. der dritten/ 1. der vierten und 2. der fünfften Grösse sind/ und theils an dem Schnabel und Haubt/ theils an dem Leib und Flügeln zu sehen. Dieser Vogel wird dem ♄ und auch der ♀ zugeeignet/ stehet unferne dem Becher und der ♍.

G. III. HONI · SOIT · QUI · MAL · Y · PENSE · REX.

DIEU ET MON DROIT

No 2

ROWLEY & Co.

To famed Moorfeilds I dayly doe repair, Kill worms cure Itch & make ye Ladyes fair.

DESIGNERS
AND
PUBLISHERS

22

1

ARMANINO, Fratelli

Pack of 52 standard whist cards, French suits, double-ended, published by Fratelli Armanino, Genoa, 1908. In case with maker's name etc, backs with a diaper of dots and squares in blue. Lettered on the court cards with name and address of makers, on the Duty Ace of Hearts with makers' name and address and date *12 Dic 1908*.
Colour lithographs. Each 8.7 × 5.6 cm (CR)
E.1550.1-52—1926
Given by Mr Arthur Myers Smith

2

BACKOFEN, Johann Ernst (worked 1st quarter of 19th century)

Cards (17), from a pack published by JE Backofen, Nuremberg, early 19th century. Backs with seaweed pattern. Lettered on the Deuce of Hearts *Johan Ernst*; on the Deuce of Bells *Backofen*, and on the Deuce of Acorns *In Nürnberg*. Duty paid stamp on Deuce of Hearts.
Woodcuts, coloured by hand. Each 8.8 × 7.1 cm (CR)
E.6308.1-17—1910 (no.1344-1872)

3

BACKOFEN, Johann Matthias (worked late 18th century)

Pack of 40 cards (Ace, Two to Seven and three court cards in four suits).
The court cards, standing figures.
Published by JM Backofen, Nuremberg, late 18th century. [G.M. 1615-1655] Backs with small diaper diamond pattern.
Lettered on the Knave of Spades *Verfertiget von Ioh.Matth.Backofen in Nürnberg*.
Engravings and colour stencil. Each 8.4 × 6 cm
E.6300.1-40—1910

4

BACKOFEN, Wilhelm (worked early 19th century)

Cards (21), from a pack published by Wilhelm Backofen, Nuremberg, early 19th century. Backs with random blue pattern.
Lettered on Deuce of Hearts *Wilhelm*; on Deuce of Bells *Backofen*, and on Deuce of Acorns *in Nürnberg*. Duty paid stamp on Deuce of Hearts.
Woodcuts, coloured by hand. Each 8.7 × 7.4 cm (CR)
E.6307.1-21—1910 (no.1343-1872)

5

BALLER (or BALLEK), M

Cards (32), standard, published by M Baller, Prague, late 19th century. Backs with plaid pattern in black.
[O'Donoghue, No.82]
Lettered on Deuce of Acorns *M Baller* (or *Ballek*); on the Deuce of Acorns *Prag*. Duty stamp (double-headed eagle) on Deuce of Acorns.
Woodcuts and colour stencil. Each 9.6 × 5.7 cm.
no.29569.P.1-32

6

BANCKS Brothers (worked 2nd quarter of 19th century)

Pack of 52 cards, standard, full length figures, published by Bancks Brothers, c.1830. Backs plain pink.
Lettered on Duty Ace of Spades *Duty One Shilling Bancks Brothers Successors To Hunt & Sons*.
Woodcuts and colour stencil, the Ace of Spades engraved. Each 9.3 × 6.4 cm.
E.825.1-52—1937
Given by Mr LJ Frost

The Ace of Spades is printed from the same plate, with lettering changed, as the Duty card of another pack, E.695—1950, see GOODALL, Charles & Son.

7

BARLOW, Francis (c.1626-1704), After

'The Popish Plot'. Pack of 52 politico-historical cards, dealing with the Titus Oates conspiracy and the murder of Sir Edmund Berry Godfrey. By an unidentified engraver after Francis Barlow. [Keller, ENG 77 (same back pattern) Willshire, E.186-188; Hoffmann, 72a, 72c] Backs with geometrical pattern.
Lettered with captions and numerals.
Engravings. Each 8.8 × 5.2 cm.
nos.20366.1-52

The designs for this pack are in an album of drawings in the British Museum (E Hodnett, *Francis Barlow First Master of English Book Illustration*, London 1978, pp.25, 26). The cards were available either as a pack or in two broadsheets 'fit to adorn studies and houses', at a cost of 8d each.
  There are several variations of this pack. An advertisement in *The True Domestick Intelligencer*, No.50, 26 December 1679, lists what is possibly the second of a series dealing with Popish Plots, 'printed and sold by Robert Walton at the Globe on the north side of St. Paul's Churchyard near the West End, where you may have a pack for eightpence of the very best; you

may have them in sheets to adorn studios and houses'. (*Catalogue of the Collection of Playing Cards of Various Ages and Countries formed by Henry D Phillips*, London, 1903, No.236.) Packs were also published by Jonathan Wilkins and Jacob Sampson, c.1679.
See also ANONYMOUS: ENGLISH, last quarter of 17th century, and FACSIMILE & REPRODUCTION PACKS

8
BENDA & Co., Anton (worked 3rd quarter of 19th century)

Cards (40), from a standard pack of 52, courts full length, published by A Benda & Co., Coburg & London, c.1865. Backs with diaper dot pattern in red. Lettered on Ace of Spades with maker's name and address.
Woodcuts and colour stencil, the Ace of Spades engraved. Each 9.9 × 6.6 cm (CR)
E.269.1-40—1951
Given by Mr AV Thais

9
BIERMANS, Leonard, S.A.

Jeep. Cards (52, and Joker) for whist, standard, French suits, courts double-ended, Aces with caricatures of Eisenhower, De Gaulle, Stalin and Montgomery, the Joker, a caricature of Hitler. Published by L Biermans, S.A., Turnhout, Belgium, 1943-44. Backs with a Jeep car. In slip-case, with matching pictorial decoration, lettered with title, maker's name etc.
Colour offset lithography. Each 8.4 × 5.7 cm (CR)
E.29.1-53—1951

10
BIGGS, Leslie (born 1944), and other artists

Pack of cards (68) for the game of Snap, designed and printed by 34 artists (staff and students) at the Royal College of Art, London, c.1975. In a box with rules for the game, list of contributors etc pasted inside the lid, and a card, back upwards, pasted on the outside of the lid.
Numbered in red on the inside bottom of the box *R.C.A. 39/120*.
Lithography and screenprinting, some coloured (the backs screenprinted). Each 14.9 × 11.7 cm.; in box 15.7 × 12.6 cm.
E.36.1-68—1976
Given by the Printmaking Department of the Royal College of Art

11
BLAKE, Peter (born 1932)

Snap II. Incorporating cards (5), from a pack of 56 Snap cards, published by John Jacques & Son Ltd, c.1885. Circ. 501—1963. See also JACQUES, John & Son Ltd, E.552.1-54—1971
Exhibitions: Tate Gallery, No.35

12
BLOME, Richard (worked late 17th century)

Pack of 52 heraldic cards, issued by Richard Blome, c.1677. [O'Donoghue, No.52; Hargrave, pp.173,174; Morley, pp.147,148; Keller, ENG 93]
Backs plain.
Lettered with captions etc, and on the Three of Hearts with dedication to the Duke of Albemarle by R Blome.
Engravings. Each 9.2 × 6.1 cm. nos.20367.1-52

A pack in the Guildhall Library and Art Gallery [No.233 (J.B.)], dated c.1675, has an extra card, probably unique, showing a half-length, winged female figure floating in the air, holding a drapery lettered 'Armoriall Cards, comprising in a "Methodical Method the Whole Body of Heraldry, with rules the better to attaine to the knowledge thereof." By Ric.Blome sold by Hen. Broome at the Gun in St. Pauls Churchyard. Where the said cards may be had in colours'. [This title-page not mentioned by Schreiber]
A facsimile pack was issued to members of the WCPM in 1888.

13
BORIOTA, G (worked last quarter of 19th century)

Pack of 50 cards, full-length figures in pseudo-historical costumes, published by Luigi Adami, Florence, 1882. Backs with blue marble pattern. With fragmentary wrapper. [Keller, ITA sheet 283]
Lettered on wrapper with maker's name and address etc and on Ace of Hearts with Duty stamp and *Fabrica Adami Firenze*.
Woodcuts, coloured by hand. Each 9.9 × 6.5 cm.
E.1836.1-52—1885

14

Another pack, backs red marble
E.1830.1-52—1885

15

BREPOLS, S.A., Possibly by (worked 20th century)

Pack of 52 cards and Joker, standard, courts double-ended, the Joker a Punch figure, scattering cards from his shoulder bag. Backs with conventional scrolling leaf and medallion pattern. (?) Published by Brepols S.A., Turnhout, Belgium. Lettered on the Joker *Joker*.
Colour offset lithography. Each 8.7 × 5.6 cm (CR)
E.920-974—1934

16

Pack of 52 cards and Joker, courts double-ended, the Joker with cap and bells, holding the four Aces. (?) published by Brepols S.A., Turnhout, Belgium, 20th century. Backs with interlocking circles and zig-zag border pattern.
Colour off-set lithography. Each 8.9 × 5.9 cm (CR)
E.1382-1434—1934

17

Pack of 52 cards and Joker, standard, double-ended, the Joker flying above a town, the Aces each with two topographical scenes. (?) published by Brepols S.A., Turnhout, Belgium, 20th century. Backs with pattern of four dogs' heads, the chains of the collars interlinked.
Lettered on the Aces with place names and *Déposé*. Lettered on the Joker *The Jolly Joker Made in Belgium*.
Colour offset lithography. Each 9.2 × 6.1 cm (CR)
E.1329-1381—1934

18

BROTHERTON,– (worked early 19th century)

Duty stamp (Ace of Spades). 1803. Lettered *G.III.Rex. Exportation Brotherton*. Numbered *14*.
Engraving. Cut to 9.8 × 6.6 cm.
E.853—1950
Given by Mrs IW Bailey

19

BRUCK, Pet. (? worked late 19th century)

Cards (21), the numerals I to XXI from a Bavarian 'animal' tarot pack, published by Pet. Bruck, Luxembourg, (?) late 19th century. Backs blue and yellow blotch.
Lettered on the 'harlequin' card *V. Quarante / Pet. Bruck Luxemburg* (twice).
Woodcuts and colour stencil. Each 10.5 × 5.9 cm.
E.1634.1-21—1926
Given by Mr ALB Ashton

O'Donoghue, No.130, describes a pack by this maker, the backs with 'a small red pattern', the same dimensions, 'modern' (i.e. late 19th century).

20

BÜRGERS, Johann Peter (worked early 19th century)

Wrapper. Early 19th century. German. [Keller, GER 101]
Lettered *Franzoesische Piquet Karten von JP Bürgers in Cöln*.
Woodcut, printed in blue. Size of sheet 20.4 × 25.7 cm.
(Unregistered)

21

'CASSANDRE', A M (pseudonym of Adolphe MOURON) (born 1901)

Pack of 52 cards and two Jokers, non-standard, double-ended, plus title card, published by Hermès, Paris, 1950. Backs with floral panel in red. In red slip-case.
Lettered on the title-card *Composé Par A.M. Cassandre Pour Hermès-Paris Ce Jeu De Cartes A été Imprimé Par Draeger-Freres Made in France*, on Ace of Clubs *Hermès Paris*, on Joker *Joker*.
Colour half-tone blocks. Each 9.1 × 6.4 cm (CR)
E.667.1-55—1951

Keller, FRA 352 describes an earlier pack (1948), (with slight variations, for Poker, as well as above). According to Keller, the designer's real name was Jean Marie Mouron.

22

COISSIEUX, Jacques (worked 2nd half of 18th century)

Sheet of cards with Spanish suit signs, published by Jacques Coissieux, Romans, 1772-1795. Modern impression.
Woodcuts. Size of sheet 35.8 × 32.3 cm.
No.16295 (E.704—1913)

23
COLEMAN, William Stephen (1829-1904)
Design for the decoration of the back of a card: a Japanese woman picking fruit. c.1876.
Line block and colour lithography. 9 × 6 cm.
E.2463—1953
Bequeathed by Tristram Little

24
CRATO, J F (worked c.1810)
Cards (29), the courts full length figures, the numerals with putti engaged in various pursuits. Published by JH Crato, Lüneburg, c.1810. Backs with paste paper pattern.
Lettered on Deuce of Acorns *JF Crato in Lüneburg*.
Woodcuts. Each 10 × 6.2 cm.
E.6298.1-29—1910 (979-1872)

Repr. Claus D Grupp, *Spielkarten und ihre Geschichte . . .*, Leinfelden, 1973, pl. on p.45 (col.)

25
CRESWICK, Thomas (worked 1st half of 19th century)
Cards (40) from a pack of 52, standard, full length figures, published by Thomas Creswick, c.1820-28. Backs plain.
Lettered on Duty Ace of Spades *G. IV Rex. Duty One Shilling And Sixpence. Thomas Creswick*.
Woodcut and colour stencil, the Ace of Spades engraved. Each 9.4 × 6.4 cm.
E.270.1-40—1951
Given by Mr AV Thais

26
'CROWQUILL', Alfred (pseudonym of Alfred Henry FORRESTER) (1804-1872)
Pack of 52 transformation cards, the numerals of each suit with caricature heads, the courts also caricatures, published by Reynolds & Sons, London, c.1845. Backs, dotted star pattern. [Hargrave, p.217; Keller, ENG 148]
Lettered on Ace of Spades with maker's name and *Duty One Shilling*.
Colour lithographs. Each 9.2 × 6.4 cm., Ace of Spades engraved.
E.3630-3681—1915
Given by Miss JM Charles

Repr. F Hicklin, *Playing Cards*, HMSO, London, 1976 (cover illust. Jack of Clubs)

27
DAVELUY, Fabrica De (worked 3rd quarter of 19th century)
Cards (48), the courts, single figures of rulers and warriors of Europe, Africa, America and Asia; the numerals, Cups, Swords, Batons and Coins.
Published by Fabrica de Daveluy, Bruges, 3rd quarter of 19th century.
Backs with seaweed pattern.
Lettered on Ace of Money *Fabrica De Daveluy Bruges Belgica* and *Asia*, and on the remaining Aces with names of countries.
Colour lithographs. Each 9.1 × 5.5 cm.
E.460.1-48—1973

28

Pack of 52 cards, courts double-ended, standard, published by Daveluy, Bruges, late 19th century. Backs with dotted circle pattern. In slip-case with Jack of Clubs on front.
Lettered on Knave of Hearts with maker's name, on Ace of Spades *Dépose* and on Ace of Clubs *Cartes Brevetées*.
Colour lithographs. Each 8.8 × 5.9 cm (CR)
E.1544.1-52—1926
Given by Mr Arthur Myers Smith

29
DE LA RUE & Co (worked 2nd half of 19th century)
Amalgamated with Charles GOODALL & Son Ltd, c.1925, *q.v.*
See also JONES, Owen, TOWNROE, Reuben.

Pack of 52 cards, published by De La Rue & Co, to celebrate the Great Exhibition of 1851, with the coat of arms of Queen Victoria and Prince Albert embossed in gold on the backs. First published by De La Rue, London, c.1840.
Lettered on Duty Ace of Spades London *De La Rue & Co By His Majesty's Letters Patent* etc.
Colour lithographs. Each 8.9 × 5.8 cm.
E.133.1-52—1969
Given by Miss Cécile Desgratoulet

A similar pack was issued by De La Rue c.1830 to celebrate the coronation of

George IV (Phillips Collection, No.203)
Illust. *Festival Number of the De La Rue
Journal*, No.13, July 1951, f.p.25. The
coat of arms is also used to decorate the
cover.

30

Pack of 52 cards, non-standard, double-
ended, the figures in period costumes,
published by Thomas De La Rue,
London and Paris, 3rd quarter of 19th
century. Backs plain yellow.
Lettered in an oval device on Ace of
Spades with maker's name and address.
Colour lithographs. Each 8.8 × 5.7 cm.
E.509.1-52—1952

31

Pack of 52 cards, standard, courts
double-ended, published by De La Rue
& Co, London, c.1862-70. Backs dec-
orated with a conventional floral pattern
in red, blue, green and gold.
Lettered on Ace of Spades with maker's
name etc.
Colour lithographs. Each 9.3 × 6.5 cm.
E.2584.1-52—1917
Given by Mr Arthur Myers Smith

32

Pack of 52 cards, standard, courts
double-ended, published by De La Rue
& Co, London, c.1860. Backs with
trailing stems of Tudor roses.
Lettered on Duty Ace of Spades *Duty One
Shilling London De La Rue & Co By His
Majesty's Royal Letters Patent*.
Colour lithographs. Each 9.4 × 6.4 cm.
E.92.1-52—1961
Given by Mrs Currie Martin

These cards, once the property of Henry
Fawcett, Post Master General, were
given to him by the donor's husband,
the late Professor Currie Martin.
Fawcett, who was blinded in a shooting
accident in 1858, cut and embossed
them for his own use.

33

Pack of 52 standard, double-ended
cards, issued to commemorate the
Golden Jubilee of Queen Victoria,
published by De La Rue & Co, London,
1887. Backs with the Royal coat of arms
and emblems representing the Colonies.
Backs lettered *Jubilee of Her Majesty Queen
Victoria 1887 Empress of India God Save
the Queen* etc.
Lettered on Ace of Spades with maker's
name.
Colour letterpress. Each 8.7 × 6.2 cm.
E.77.1-52—1951
Given by Mr FS Bolam

34

Pack of 52 cards, standard, courts
double-ended, published by De La Rue
& Co, London, 1898. Backs with
guilloche and acanthus leaf pattern.
Lettered on Ace of Spades with maker's
trademark and name.
Colour lithographs. Each 8.9 × 6.2 cm
(CR)
E.348C.1-52—1955
Given by Mrs EGB Finney

The pack was included in a 'Jeu de Nain
Jaune', E.348,348A—1955, also given
by the above-named donor.

35

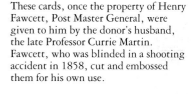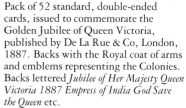

Pack of 52 cards, standard, double-
ended, and a Joker, published by De La
Rue & Co, London, 1917. Backs with a
moresque pattern in red. In slip-case
with pictorial title label.
Lettered on the slip-case *Flexette Playing
Cards* and with maker's name etc.
Lettered on Ace of Spades with
trademark, name and address etc. Joker
lettered *The Joker*.
Colour lithographs. Each 8.8 × 5.7 cm
(CR)
E.452.1-53—1918
Given by Mr Arthur Myers Smith

36

Packs (2), each of 32 cards and Joker, for the game of Bézique, published by Thomas De La Rue & Co Ltd, and Charles Goodall & Son Ltd, 1927. With score markers (4), and a booklet of rules for playing Bézique and Rubicon Bézique. In box with pictorial lid incorporating Goodall's trademark. Backs with classical floral pattern in red. Lettered on Ace of Spades with Goodall's name and address.
Colour lithographs. Each 8.9 × 5.8 cm; in box 11 × 14.8 cm.
E.1—1985 (box); E.1.1-69—1985
Given by Miss JD Hamilton

The 'Royal Game of Bézique' and 'Rubicon Bézique', which is a later version, is played with packs in which the lowest numeral card is seven. The game originated in the south of France and in Germany, where it is known as 'Penuchle'. It was introduced into England by Dr Pole in 1861, and in 1869 it suddenly became very popular and was taken up by the clubs in London and in Paris.

37

DELLA BELLA, Stefano (1610-1664), Copies after

Cards (15) from a pack of 52 geographical cards; the figures emblematic of the various countries are copies after Della Bella, on a pack first published by Jean Desmaret in 1644, republished by N Le Clerc in 1698. This edition has German suit signs and is lettered in German. German, late 17th or early 18th century. [Bierdimpfle, No.17; De Vesne pl.542; Keller, GER 451 (similar)] Backs with a red stipple pattern.
Lettered in German with names of countries, descriptions etc.
Engravings. Each 10.2 × 6 cm.
E.6301.1-15—1910 (no.1337-1872)

38

Cards (29), from a pack of 52 geographical cards, the figures emblematic of the various countries are copies *in reverse* after Della Bella, on a pack first published by Jean Desmaret in 1644, republished by N Le Clerc in 1698. This edition has German suit signs added and is lettered in German. German, late 17th or early 18th century. [Bierdimpfle, No.17; De Vesne pl.542; Keller, GER 451 (similar)] Backs plain. Lettered with names of countries, description etc in German.
Engraving and letterpress. Each 10.3 × 6 cm.
E.6303.1-29—1910 (no.1339-1872)

39

Cards (39), from a pack of historical cards, the figures are copies *in reverse* of the engravings on a pack entitled 'Cartes des Rois de France' by Stefano Della Bella, first published by Jean Desmaret in 1644, republished by N Le Clerc in 1698. This edition has German suit signs added and the figures are re-titled with the names of Roman emperors and other ancient rulers. German, late 17th or early 18th century. [Bierdimpfle, No.41; De Vesne pl.648; Keller, GER 451 (similar)] Backs plain.
Lettered with titles, descriptions etc in German.
Engravings. Each 9.6 × 5.4 cm.
E.6304.1-39—1910 (no.1340-1872)

40

DELLAROCCA, Carlo (died post 1824), After

Pack of 78 tarot cards, copy of that engraved by C Dellarocca, published by Gumppenberg, Milan, c.1840. Backs with circular dotted pattern. [Hargrave, pp.231, 232 (stamp dated 1842); O'Donoghue, No.7 (dated c.1820); BN, No.54 (copy); Keller, ITA 36 (dated c.1840); Guildhall, J.B. 505 (c.1820)] Lettered on the King of Batons *Faba. Di Gumppenburg Milano C. Dellarocca inc.* and with the Lombardy Duty stamp etc. Also stamped *E. Dotti Mil.*

Engravings and colour stencil. Each
10.6 × 5.3 cm.
nos.15864.1-77 & 51a

The original designs for these cards are
in the British Museum (Nos.1896-1-29-
1).

41

DONDORF, Firma Bernhard J (1833-1933)

Tarot pack of 78 cards, the courts
representing famous people, and the
Aces famous buildings of Europe. French
suit signs, double-ended. No.244,
published by B Dondorf, Frankfurt-on-
Main, 1887. Backs with classical design.
In slip-case with same design. [O'Don-
oghue, 118; Keller, GER, 616
(No.245); DH & MD pp.70,71]
Lettered on Aces and court cards with
names of people and buildings, and *B
Dondorf Francfort*. Stamped on the Ace of
Hearts with Duty stamp.
Colour lithographs and stencil. Each
10.7 × 5.9 cm.
E.462.1-78—1973

42

Whist cards (51, from a pack of 52),
courts double-ended, French suit signs,
the numerals made into transformations
by an unidentified English artist.
Published by B Dondorf, Frankfurt-on-
Main, c.1880-90. Backs with honey-
suckle stems [DH & MD pp. 86, 87]
Lettered on the Knave of Clubs *B
Dondorf Frankfurt a.M.* Inscribed in ink
on several of the numerals with captions,
Vote for Gladstone; *Oyley Carte Theatre* etc.
Colour lithographs, pen and red and
black inks. Each 8.4 × 5.7 cm (CR)
E.833.1-51—1969
Given by Mr PL Bushe-Fox

43

'Baronesse' Whist, No.160. Pack of 52
cards, produced by B Dondorf,
Frankfurt-on-Main, 1899. French suit
signs and courts double-ended. Backs,
roses on a diagonal gold ground. [Keller,
GER 525 (162); DH & MD
pp. 106, 107]
Lettered on Knave of Clubs *B Dondorf
Frankfurt a/M.*
Colour lithographs. Each 9.2 × 6 cm
(CR)
E.1437.1-52—1979
Given by Mr MacFarlane

44

Miniature Patience cards (40, from a
pack of 52), the courts and Aces
representing the four Continents, French
suits, double-ended. Published by
Dondorf, Frankfurt-on-Main, before
1870. Backs pictorial (birds and a
fountain) [DH & MD, p.68]
Lettered on the Aces with place names
etc, on the courts with publisher's name.
Colour litho-engravings. Each 6.4 ×
4.3 cm.
E.505.1-40—1961
Given by Mr PL Bushe-Fox

The courts and Aces are identical to
Keller, GER 390, except that they are
slightly smaller and have no indices. The
backs are the same but pink instead of
blue.

45

DUBOIS, JT (worked 1st quarter of 19th century)

Cards (44, from a pack of 52, and one,
the Four of Clubs, from a companion
pack), French suit signs and Paris
pattern courts, published by JT Dubois,
Liége. Flemish, 1st quarter of 19th
century. [Willshire Fl.104 (similar pack
c.1813); Supplement vol. Fl.271
(difference in names on court cards);
Keller, BEL 14 (similar, c.1790)] Backs,
chain and diamond dot pattern.
Lettered on the King of Spades *JT Dubois*
and on the Knave of Clubs *A Liége.*
Woodcuts and colour stencil. Each 8.5
× 5.6 cm.
E.1668.1-45—1948
Given by Mr CTB Simmons

46

DURAND, (?) L (worked 18th century)

Printing block for cards (16), full length
figures, no suit signs, and two blank
cartouches. Also a modern impression
from the block. By (?) L Durand, Liége,
18th century.
Lettered on the Ace of (?)Roses *L{?}
Durand A'Liége.*
Size of block, approx. 11.4 × 29.2 ×
5 cm.
E.470A,B-1916

47
DURAND, F (worked early 16th century)
Sheets (2) of cards, each containing eight subjects, four Kings and four Queens bearing titles of legendary and historical personages: Charlemaigne; Bersabee [*Bethsabée*]; Priam; Palas; David etc. Rouen or Lyons, early 16th century. Signed on 'la grants baslive' *F*. Woodcuts, coloured by hand. Size of sheet 18.9 × 27.6 cm.
E.1255,1256—1916

48
FETSCHER, – (worked (?) late 18th century)
Pearwood block, cut on both sides, and a sheet of cards (36), standard suits, with pipers, drummers, swordsmen, pikemen and Kings; on the Ten of Leaves, a fox, on the Nine of Leaves, a camel. Sheet of cards (10), printed from reverse of block, with five Knaves of Money and five Kings of (?) Houses. Munich, (?) late 18th century.
Lettered on the Knaves of Money on the reverse sheet *Fetscher*, and in their axeheads *F*.
Woodblock. 30 × 19 × 5 cm.
no.225–1872

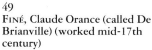

49
FINÉ, Claude Orance (called De Brianville) (worked mid-17th century)
Cards (47) from a pack of 52, first published by CO Finé, Lyons, c.1658. [O'Donoghue 129 (later pack); Morley, pp.107-109 (c.1660, illustr.); Keller, FRA 283; Hoffmann No.66a (illustr.)] With arms of States, Sovereigns, Princes and Nobles of Europe. Backs, a diaper pattern of crosses within hexagons. Lettered with descriptive texts etc. King of Clubs with arms of Pope Alexander VII (1655-1667).
Engravings, some coloured by hand. Each 9 × 6.5 cm.
E.1577.1-47—1885

50
FOURNIER, Braulio (worked 3rd quarter of 19th century)
Ombre cards (40), standard (except that the numerals of batons have branches of leaves), published by B Fournier, Burgos, c.1870. Backs with tangled pattern of blue lines. Fragmentary wrapper.
Lettered on Four of Money with maker's name and address, and on Four of Cups *Premiado En Varias Exposiciones*
Colour lithographs. Each 9.4 × 5.8 cm.
nos.29432.1-40
Given by Senor José Joaquin de Carreras

51
Ombre cards (40), standard, published by B Fournier, Burgos, c.1870. Backs decorated as above. In blue pictorial wrapper numbered 3.
Lettered on Ace of Money and Four of Cups with maker's name and address, on Ace of Cups *Burgos* and on Four of Money *Premiado En Varias Exposiciones Clase Tercera No.3 Vitela De 3A*.
Colour lithographs. Each 9.3 × 5.9 cm.
nos.29433.1-40
Given by Senor José Joaquin de Carreras

52
FOURNIER, Heraclio (worked 3rd quarter of 19th century)
Cards (40, from a pack of 48), standard, published by H Fournier, Vitoria, Spain, c.1880. Backs decorated in brown as previous two packs by B Fournier. In pictorial wrapper numbered 6.
Lettered on Four of Money and of Cups with maker's name and address, and *No.3*. On Ace of Money *Premiado en la Exposicion Paris de 1878*.
Colour lithographs. Each 9.4 × 5.9 cm.
nos.29434.1-40
Given by Senor José Joaquin de Carreras

53
FRANKENBERGER, Jakob (worked 19th century)
Cards (12), standard, court figures standing in French style, Bavarian, published by J Frankenberger, Landshut, 1760-80. [Bierdimpfle, No.54; Keller, GER 26] 19th century impressions.
Lettered on Knave of Clubs *J* (within the pike blade), *L H* (within the shield) and *Jacob Freng.Berg*. On King of Diamonds *Lonzhut*.
Woodcuts. Each 8.8 × 5.9 cm.
E.591.1-12—1885
Given by the Bavarian National Museum, Munich

54
FULLADOSA y Ca (worked 3rd quarter of 19th century)
Pack of 48 cards, non-standard, courts full length figures representing Europe, Africa, Asia and America, published by Fulladosa y Ca, Barcelona, 1872. [Hargrave, p.255]
Backs with diagonal plaid pattern. (Hargrave, p.255)
Lettered on Aces with names of continents, and on Four of Cups *De Una Hoja. Por Fulladosa Y Ca. Barna*.
Woodcuts and colour stencil. Each 9.2 × 5.7 cm.
nos.29436.1-48

55

FULLER, Samuel & Joseph (c. 1808-1828)

Duty Stamp. 1808 (Ace of Spades)
Lettered *G.III Rex. Saml. & Josh. Fuller.*
Numbered *13*.
Engraving. Cut to 10.8 × 6.2 cm.
E.851—1950
Given by Mrs IW Bailey

56

Duty wrapper. Blank space for blind stamp.
Lettered with regulations etc and *Saml. & Josh. Fuller. Stamp Office A.* etc.
Numbered *3*.
Engraving, printed in red. Cut to (octagonal) 14.9 × 10.4 cm.
E.854—1950
Given by Mrs IW Bailey

57

GLANZ, Joseph

Pack of 36 cards, standard, courts double-ended, published by Joseph Glanz, Vienna, 19th century. Backs with zig-zag pattern. In wrapper No.46. Lettered on the Four of Bells *I.Glanz.Wien.* and on the Seven of Hearts *Glanz Josef Wien* and with the K.K.Kartemstempel 1.
Woodcuts and colour stencil. Each 9.9 × 5.9 cm.
no.29569.G.1-36

Duplicate pack: no.29569.H.1-36

58

Pack of 36 cards, standard, courts full length, published by Joseph Glanz, Vienna, 19th century. Backs with zig-zag pattern. In wrapper No.52. Lettered on the Deuce of Acorns *Jos. Glanz In Wien*, on the Eight of Hearts *Glanz Josef Wien* (partly obliterated) and with the K.K.Kartenstempel 1.
Woodcuts and colour stencil. Each 10 × 6.2 cm.
nos.29569.J.1-36

Duplicate pack, with 4 cards missing: nos.29569.K.1-32

59

Cards (32, from a pack of 36), standard, courts full length, published by Joseph Glanz, Vienna, third quarter of 19th century. [? O'Donoghue 89] Backs with acorn and trellis pattern. (illustr.) In wrapper No.54, with address Kohlmarkt, No.20
Lettered on the Deuce of Acorns *Josef Glanz*, on the Deuce of Hearts *Wien*, and on the Eight of Bells *Glanz Josef In Wien*, and with the K.K.Kartenstempel 1.
Woodcuts and colour stencil. Each 9.5 × 5.6 cm.
nos.29569.L.1-32

Duplicate packs (imperfect).
nos.29569.M,N

60

Cards (32, from a pack of 36), courts full length in pseudo-historic costume, published by Joseph Glanz, Vienna, mid-19th century. Backs with a paste paper pattern.
Lettered on the Seven of Bells *Joseph* (the J reversed) *Glanz in Wien.*, and on the Seven of Hearts *Glanz Josef In Wien*, and with the double-headed eagle stamp No.10.
Woodcuts and colour stencil. Each 9.2 × 5.7 cm.
nos.29569.Q.1-32

61

Feine Trapulier. Pack of 36 trappola cards, double-ended, published by Joseph Glanz, Vienna, late 19th century. Backs with a zig-zag pattern. With wrapper No.21 (altered in ink to 27), bearing the Kohlmarkt address.
Lettered on the Ace of Batons *Jos. Glanz in Wien* (twice) and with the Schutzmarke (twice), on the Seven of Roses *Fabrik: IV.Kleinschmidgasse No 3* Wien, and on the Ten of Roses stamped *Glanz Josef Wien* and with the K.K.Kartenstempel No.1.
Woodcuts and colour stencil. Each 12.5 × 6.1 cm.
no.29569.I.1-36

62

Militär-Tarock. Pack of 54 cards, the court cards depict historical characters such as Richard Coeur de Lion, and the numerals military subjects and portraits of generals and emperor Franz Josef I. Published by J Glanz, Vienna, 1873. [Keller, AUS 211; Guildhall, No.594 (3rd state, c.1865); Koplan 305 (c.1854)] Backs with dot and asterisk pattern. In wrapper with camp scene, and address Niederlage am Kohlmarkt No.20, and with a stamp recording that a medal was won at the Vienna World Exhibition in 1873.

Lettered with names of characters etc.
Stamped on the Ace of Hearts *Glanz Josef in Wien*, and with the
K.K.Kartenstempel No.1.
Colour lithographs. Each 10.2 ×
5.5 cm
no.29569.F.1-54

63

Pack of 36 trappola cards, double-ended, published by Joseph Glanz, Vienna, 19th century. Backs with zig-zag pattern. In wrapper No.37 with address Kohlmarkt No.20, and Vienna Exhibition stamp 1873.
Lettered on the Ace of Batons *Jos:Glanz In Wien* and with stamp
K.K.Kartenstempel 1.
Colour lithographs. Each 10.4 ×
5.5 cm.
nos.29569.D.1-36

Duplicate pack: no.29569.E.1-36

64

Piquet cards (32), double-ended courts, French suits, published by Joseph Glanz, Vienna, mid 19th century. Backs with same pattern as above. In wrapper No.6.
Lettered on the Knave of Spades *Josef Glanz*, on the Knave of Hearts *In Wien* and on the Ace of Hearts *Glanz Josef [in] Wien*, and with the K.K.Kartenstempel 1.
Woodcuts and colour stencil. Each 8.4 × 5.4 cm.
nos.29569.A.1-32

65

Pack of 36 cards, standard, full length, published by Joseph Glanz, Vienna, 19th century. Backs with zig-zag pattern. In wrapper No.16, with address Kohlmarkt No.20.
Lettered on the Deuce of Acorns *Feine deutsche Karten Niederlage Kohlmarkt N.279 Jos Glanz In Wien*, on the Seven of Hearts *Glanz Josef In Wien* and stamped K.K.Kartenstempel 1.
Woodcuts and colour stencil. Each 9.9 × 5.9 cm.
no.29569.B.1-36

Duplicate pack: no.29569.C.1-36

66

GOMBAU, Vicente (worked 3rd quarter of 19th century)

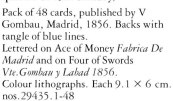

Pack of 48 cards, published by V Gombau, Madrid, 1856. Backs with tangle of blue lines.
Lettered on Ace of Money *Fabrica De Madrid* and on Four of Swords *Vte.Gombau y Labad 1856*.
Colour lithographs. Each 9.1 × 6 cm.
nos.29435.1-48

67

GOODALL, Charles & Son (worked c.1830-   )

Pack of 52 cards, standard, full length figures, published by C Goodall & Son, c.1835. Backs with quatrefoil and interlace diaper in blue.
Lettered on Ace of Spades *Goodall. Duty One Shilling*.
Woodcuts and colour stencil. Each 9.1 × 6.4 cm. (Ace of Spades engraved)
E.695.1-52—1950
Given by Mr AG Walker

The Ace of Spades is printed from the same plate, with lettering changed, as the Duty card of another pack by Bancks Brothers (E.825—1937)

68

Pack of 52 cards, standard, courts double-ended, and Joker, published by C Goodall & Son Ltd, London, c.1875. Backs with interwoven small shapes in red.
Lettered on Ace of Spades with maker's name etc.
Colour lithographs. Each 9.3 × 6.6 cm.
E.1821.1-52—1917
Given by Mr Arthur Myers Smith

69

Pack of 52 cards, standard, double-ended courts, published by C Goodall & Son Ltd, c.1898. Backs with a design composed of bicycle parts, including handlebars entwined with oak leaves.
Lettered on Ace of Spades with maker's name, trademark etc.
Colour letterpress. Each 9.2 × 6.4 cm (CR)
E.348B.1-52—1955
Given by Mrs EGB Finney

This pack was included in a 'Jeu du Nain Jaune' by De La Rue, also given by the above-named donor, E.348,348A—1955.

70

Perseverance Series. Pack of 52 cards, standard, courts double-ended and Joker, published by C Goodall & Son Ltd, London, early 20th century. Backs with a vine leaf pattern in blue. In slip-case with title and trademark on front, back with vine leaf pattern.
Lettered on Ace of Spades with maker's name etc.
Colour lithographs. Each 8.9 × 6.4 cm (CR)
E.1822.1-53—1917
Given by Mr Arthur Myers Smith

71

Pack of 52 cards, standard, courts double-ended, and a Joker, published by C Goodall & Son Ltd, London, c.1910-20. Backs with arms of the Army and Navy Club, printed on pink ground. Lettered on Ace of Spades with maker's name, trademark etc.
Colour letterpress and lithography. Each 9 × 6.3 cm (CR)
E.813-865—1934
Given by Major CC Adams, M.C., F.S.A.

72

Pack of 52 cards, standard, courts double-ended, and two additional blank cards to show variation in the back pattern colours (green and blue). Published by C Goodall & Son, London, 1916. Backs with red floral diaper pattern.
Lettered on Ace of Spades with maker's name, trademark etc.
Colour lithographs. Each 9 × 6.3 cm (CR)
E.2585.1-54—1917
Given by Mr Arthur Myers Smith

73

Pack of 52 cards, standard, and two additional cards, Joker and the rules of scoring for contract bridge. Backs with pictorial advertisement for EO Shanks & Sons Ltd, timber merchants, of Coventry. Published by C Goodall & Son, London, c.1930.
With registered trademark on Ace of Spades.
Colour line blocks. Each 8.8 × 5.7 cm (CR)
E.3917.1-54—1983
Given by Mr Julian Litten

74

Boudoir Playing Cards. Packs (2, one unopened in Duty wrapper) of 52 cards and a Joker each, published by C Goodall & Son Ltd, Camden Town, London, N.W. Backs with a semi-nude female figure, entitled 'The Lace Shawl' and 'The Kiss' respectively. In box with title-label on lid.
Colour offset. Each 8.8 × 5.8 cm (CR); in box 10 × 13 cm.
E.1422—1986
Given by Mr CG Brooks

75

GRIMAUD, Baptiste-Paul (worked late 19th to early 20th century)

See also SIMON, F
Pack of 78 tarot cards, Italian suits, double-ended, published by B-P Grimaud, Paris, c.1880. [BN, Cat. No.115; backs with brown-mauve *opus incertum*] Backs with blue 'marble' pattern.
Lettered on Deuce of Money *BP Grimaud, Paris*. Stamped on Ace of Money with Duty stamp of the Republique (1890).
Lithographs and colour stencil. Each 10.9 × 6.3 cm (CR)
E.657-734—1934

76

Pack of 78 tarot cards, Italian suits, published by B-P Grimaud, successor to Arnoult, Paris, 1891. [Keller, FRA 159; BN Cat. No.113] Backs plain brown.
Lettered on Deuce of Money *1748 Arnoult 1748* and on the picture cards *BP Grimaud, Paris*, on the II *Junon*; V *Jupiter* and VII *V.T.*
Colour lithographs. Each 11.9 × 6.2 cm (CR)
E.579-656—1934

77

Cartes Indiennes. Pack of 52 cards, non-standard, courts single figures of Indian rulers, published by B-P Grimaud, Paris, c.1900. [Keller, FRA 368; François, pl.101 ('Jeu Turc', dated 1905)]. Backs with floral panels in red and gold.
Stamped on Ace of Clubs with blue Duty stamp of the Republique (1890).
Colour lithographs. Each 9.2 × 6.4 cm (CR)
E.1172-1223—1934

78

Pack of 52 cards, standard, courts double-ended, and Joker, published by B-P Grimaud, c.1910. [Keller, FRA 36 (backs, crosses, red)] Backs plain, pink. With laurel wreath watermark I.C.
Lettered on the courts *Charles; Judith*, etc. Knave of clubs with ornamental device lettered *1853 Administ. Des Contrib. Indir Gatteaux*. Lettered on Joker *Joker*.
Colour lithographs. Each 8.4 × 5.4 cm (CR)
E.973-1025—1934

79

Jeu Moyen Age (or Jeu Gothique). Pack of 52 cards for Whist, non-standard, courts double-ended, published by B-P Grimaud, Paris, c.1915. [Keller, FRA 373; François, pl.100 (Jeu Gothique, c.1890)] Backs, roses on red ground. Lettered on courts with titles *David*; *Pallas* etc, *BP Grimaud*. Ace of Clubs with blue Duty stamp of Republique. Colour lithographs. Each 9.2 × 6.1 cm (CR)
E.1277-1328—1934

80

Jeu Louis XV. Pack of 52 cards, non-standard, courts double-ended figures in 18th century costume, and a full length figure of a page holding a hawk (? the Joker), published by B-P Grimaud, Paris, 1920. [Keller, FRA 372; François, No.64, p.279 (facsimile pack, 1971)] Backs, floral panel with rose branch.
Colour lithographs. Each 9.2 × 6 cm (CR)
E.1224-1276—1934

The pattern was originally published in the 19th century.

81

GRÜNEWALD, F (possibly Felix Grünewald, worked c.1820-c.1840, of Nuremberg)

Comisches Lotteriespiel (Amusing Lottery game). Pack of cards (40) for a fortune-telling game, consisting of cards (20) with single character figures, the rest with mottos etc in German and in French. German, early 19th century. In slip-case with pictorial label.
Lettered on the label on the slip-case with title in German and in French and signed *F. [Grune]wald del et fec*.
Lettered in the two languages on the illustrated cards with mottos. Both sets numbered *1* to *20*.
Etchings, coloured by hand. Each 10.3 × 6.9 cm.; in case 10.6 × 7.2 cm.
E.1249.A-T—1888; E.1250.A-T—1888

81A

GUEFFIER, La Veuve (worked early 19th century)

Le Petit Oracle des Dames. Le Veritable Etteila.
Pack of 42 cards for a fortune-telling game, published by the widow Gueffier. In slip-case.
Lettered on the slip-case with title etc. and *A. Paris, chez la veuve Gueffier, Relieur, rue Galande, No.61*.
Woodcuts, coloured by hand. 9.3 × 6 cm.
29863.1-42

82

MONOGRAMMIST HGB (? worked 2nd half of 16th century)

Cards (35), modern impressions, printed from silver plates in the collection of Count Friedrich von Rothenburg. (?) 17th century.
Signed on Six of Leaves with monogram *HGB F*.
Engravings. Average size 4.7 × 3.2 cm.
E.15-50—1909

Bound in a volume entitled *Abdrücke eines vollständigen Kartenspieles auf Silberplatten gestochen von Georg Heinrich Bleich*, Munich, 1881 [Hargrave, p.98; Keller, GER 497]
    According to Thieme & Becke, the set cannot be attributed to GH Bleich, but the monogram could be that of Heinrich Godig (Goedig), 1531-1606, of Brunswick.

82A

Another set: E.15A-50A—1909

83

HALL & BANCKS (worked early 19th century)

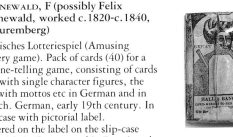

Pack of 52 cards, standard, full length figures, published by Hall & Bancks, c.1810. In original wrapper with Great Mogul portrait. In decorative octagonal box.
Lettered on Ace of Spades, Duty card, *G.III Rex* and *Hall & Bancks, Card-Makers to Her Majesty and Their Royal Highnesses the Regent and Princess* [the rest illegible], etc.
Woodcuts and colour stencil, the Ace of Spades engraved. Each 9.4 × 6.3 cm.
E.142B.1-52—1947

The box (E.142—1947), which is decorated with a representation of seven miniature cards, gardening and hunting trophies, contains three compartments, for the two packs of cards (see also Hunt & Sons, E.142A—1947), bone counters, two wooden 'fish', and two turned ivory pegs.

84

HALL & SON (1806-c.1825)

An unopened pack of 52 cards, published by Hall & Son, c.1810. In wrapper with Great Mogul portrait, engraved Duty label etc.
Lettered with maker's name and address etc. *No.25 Piccadilly London.*
E.507—1939
Given by Mrs Faith Parker

85

Another pack. In box E.403—1946
Lettered on the Duty Ace of Spades *G.III Rex* and *Hall & Son.* No.57.
E.400.1-52—1956
Given by Mr AW Pringle

Henry Hall appears as Master of the Worshipful Company of Makers of Playing Cards in 1794-95. 'The Great Mogul' was first used by C Blanchard in 1741.

86

HARDY, Henry (worked late 18th, early 19th century)

Pack of 52 cards, standard, full length figures, published by Henry Hardy, 'at the King's Arms, No.7, Old Bailey, London', between 1789-1801. With wrapper with portrait of Henry VIII.
Lettered on the Ace of Spades *G.III Rex. Hardy Sixpence Addl. Duty* etc and on the wrapper with maker's name and address and *King Henry The VIII.*
Engravings, printed in blue, and colour stencilled. Each 9.5 × 6.2 cm.
E.648.1-52—1937

Reynolds & Sons took over the blocks of 'I.Hardy' sometime after 1820.

87

HARSDÖRFER, Philip (worked late 17th century)

The Ace of Acorns. [The constellation of the Raven], from a pack of astronomical cards, produced by Harsdörfer, Nuremberg, late 17th century. With letterpress description of the constellation.
Etching. Size of card 10.2 × 5.4 cm.
E.6309—1910 (no.1345–1872)

Probably the first pack of astronomical cards, first issued by Harsdörfer in 1656, and re-issued in 1663 and 1674.
[Morley, p.93, attributes the pack to 'Endter' of Nuremberg, and repr. Ace of Hearts, King of Acorns, Six of Bells and Four of Hearts; D Hoffmann, F, p.226, commentary]

88

HART, Henry (worked early 19th century)

Pack of 52 cards, unopened in original wrapper, published by Henry Hart, Red Lion Street, Holborn, between 1801-1820. With portrait of Henry VIII on wrapper. Duty stamp, publisher's name and address etc.
Lettered on the wrapper *Henry Hart In Red Lion Street, Holborn* etc.
Woodcuts. In wrapper 9.8 × 6.4 cm.
E.649—1937

A receipt in the Department of Designs, Prints and Drawings, no.12852.2, dated 1768 is lettered *Henry Hart Card Maker at the Old Shop the Knave of Clubs in Red Lion Street Holborn Makes & Sells the best Henry 8th Great Mogul Cards &c &c.*
A Henry Hart was Master of the Worshipful Company of Makers of Playing Cards, 1763-64. Previously a John Hart, who was Master of the WCPM, 1733-34 produced the mark of *King Harry 8th* in 1737 (21 April). John Hart junior became Master in 1755-56.

The premises had been occupied in 1690 by Edward Butlin, paper-stainer and card maker, and is probably the 'Butlin', who is listed as Master in 1702-03.

89

HEATH, Adrian (born 1920), and other artists

The Deck of Cards. Pack of 52 cards, with two Jokers and a list of designers, in a slip-case with title *Deck*. Each card, the case and the reverse designed by a different artist. Published by Andrew Jones Art, London, 1979. Some signed by the artists.
Lettered with title and numbered on the case *09879.*
Colour offset. Each 9.8 × 6.3 cm.; in case 9.5 × 7.4 cm.
E.116,116a.1-54—1980
Given by Christian Neff of JPL Fine Arts

90

HENSLER, Joseph (worked 3rd quarter of 18th century)

Pack of cards (32), standard Bavarian, published by Joseph Hensler, c.1760. 19th century impressions. [Bierdimpfle, No.22; Keller, GER 171]
Lettered on the Deuce of Acorns *Ioseph Hensler Von* [the shield blank].
Woodcuts. Each 9.7 × 8.4 cm.
E.579.1-32—1885
Given by the Bavarian National Museum, Munich

91

HOLMBLADS FABRIK, LP (1820-1929)

Pack of 52 cards, standard, the court cards double-ended, pseudo-historical costumes, published by LP Holmblads Fabrik, Copenhagen, c.1865. Backs with dotted flowers on diagonal stems. Lettered on Knave of Clubs *LP Holmblads Fabrik i Kjöbenhavn.* Engravings and colour stencil. Each 9.6 × 6 cm.
E.175.1-52—1952
Given by Mr Walter Carter, C.B., C.B.E.

92

Packs (2) of 52 cards each, similar to the above, though not identical, published by LP Holmblads, Copenhagen, c.1865. Backs with dotted leaf, in red and blue respectively. With one fragmentary pictorial wrapper.
Lettered on Knave of Spades with maker's name and address.
Engravings and colour stencil. Each 9.6 × 6 cm.
E.1851.1-52—1885; E.1852.1-52—1885

93

Pack of 78 tarot cards, the courts double-ended, the numerals with French suit signs, and views, published by LP Holmblads Fabrik, Copenhagen, c.1860. Backs with dotted leaf pattern identical to above packs. [Not in Kaplan]
Lettered on Knave of Clubs *LP Holmblads Fabrik i Kjöbenhavn.*
Engravings and colour stencil. Each 11.4 × 5.9 cm.
E.1861.1-78—1885

Numerals illustr. in Catalogue of the exhibition 'Tarot, Jeu et Magie', Bibliothèque Nationale, Paris, 1984, No.108.

93A

Another pack, identical except that the backs are printed in red instead of blue.
E.1860.1-78—1885

94

HUMANES Y CA, Juan (worked 3rd quarter of 19th century)

Cards (47, from a pack of 48), the Deuce of Money missing, published by J Humanes y Ca, Madrid, 1865. Backs with tangled red lines.
Lettered on Ace of Money *Fabrica De Madrid*, and on Four of Money *Juan Humanes Y Ca. Operarios De Raimundo Garcis 1865.*
Lithographs and colour stencil. Each 9.4 × 6.2 cm.
E.383-429—1944
Given by Mrs EH Morris

The courts of a Spanish pack are without Queens.

95

HUNT & SONS (worked c.1809-c.1830)

See also BANCKS Brothers, successors to HUNT & SONS
Pack of 52 cards, standard, courts full-length figures, published by Hunt & Sons, c.1820. Backs plain. In tooled leather slip-case.
Lettered on Duty Ace of Spades with maker's name, *G.IIII Rex* and *No.23.*
Woodcuts and colour stencil, Ace of Spades engraved. Each 9.2 × 6.2 cm.
E.828.1-52—1937
Given by Mr W Thorpe Haddock

96

Another pack, in box E.403—1946. Standard, full-length figures. c.1810. Lettered on Duty Ace of Spades *G.III Rex* and *Hunt & Son, Successors to Gibson.* Numbered *137.*
E.401.1-52—1946
Given by Mr AW Pringle

97

Another pack, standard, full length figures. c.1810. Backs plain. With original Great Mogul wrapper.
Lettered on Duty Ace of Spades with maker's name *G.III.Rex* etc. Numbered *138*.
Lettered on wrapper *Hunt & Son, Card Makers to His Majesty. 53, Mortimer Street, London. Succrs. to Mattw. Gibson.*
E.506.1-53—1939
Given by Mrs Faith Parker

98

Another pack, standard, full length figures. c.1810. Backs plain. With fragmentary wrapper.
Lettered on Duty Ace of Spades *G.III Rex* and *Hunt & Sons*. Numbered *14*.
E.142A,1-52—1947

99

Another pack, standard, full length figures. c.1789-1801. Backs plain.
Lettered on Duty Ace of Spades *G.III. Rex* etc. and *Hunt*. Numbered *18*.
E.504.1-52—1939
Given by Mrs Faith Parker

100

Another pack, identical, but with one card missing.
E.505.1-51—1939
Given by Mrs Faith Parker

101

Duty stamp. 1803 (Ace of Spades).
Lettered *G.III Rex. Hunt & Sons*.
Numbered *9*.
Engraving. Cut to 8.7 × 5.4 cm.
E.849—1950
Given by Mrs IW Bailey

102

JACQUES, John & Son Ltd

The Counties of England. Pack of cards (63, including key card and card of rules), showing the chief towns and their industries, published by John Jacques & Son Ltd, Hatton Garden, London, 3rd quarter of 19th century.
Backs plain pink. [Keller ENG 61 (plain blue backs)] Letterpress names etc.
Colour wood engravings. Each 8.9 × 6.4 cm.
E.1545.1-63—1926
Given by Mr Arthur Myers Smith

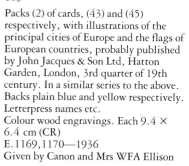

103

Packs (2) of cards, (43) and (45) respectively, with illustrations of the principal cities of Europe and the flags of European countries, probably published by John Jacques & Son Ltd, Hatton Garden, London, 3rd quarter of 19th century. In a similar series to the above.
Backs plain blue and yellow respectively.
Letterpress names etc.
Colour wood engravings. Each 9.4 × 6.4 cm (CR)
E.1169,1170—1936
Given by Canon and Mrs WFA Ellison

104

Cards (54, from a pack of 56) for the game of 'Snap', published by John Jacques & Son Ltd, 1885. Backs plain orange. With letterpress captions.
Woodcuts and colour stencil. Each 9.5 × 6 cm (CR)
E.552.1-54—1971
Given by Miss D Clover

(See also BLAKE, Peter.)

105

JENNISON-WALWORTH, Countess Charlotte von

Transformation cards (52), the court cards illustrating characters in the play by Johann Christoph Friedrich Schiller, *Die Jungfrau von Orleans* (The Maid of Orleans), 1802; the numeral cards are transformations. Published by JG Cotta, Tübingen, 1805. In original slip-case. [Keller GER 501; DH 72]
Lettered on the Ace of Clubs *A Tubinge chez JG Cotta, Libraire*.
Stipple-engravings, coloured by hand. Each 10 × 7 cm.
Nos.29178.1-52

Exhibitions: 'Die Cotta' schen Spielkarten Almanache 1805-1811', Bielefeld Deutsches Spielkarten Museum, 1968-69.

106

JONES, Owen (1809-1874), Possibly by

Cards (51, from a pack of 52), standard, courts double-ended, published by De La Rue & Co, London, c.1870. Backs with a shield of pretence, surrounded by lilies and violets.
Lettered on the Ace of Spades with maker's names and address etc.
Colour lithographs. Each 9.3 × 6.5 cm.
E.2583.1-51—1917
Given by Mr Arthur Myers Smith

Owen Jones made 173 designs for De La Rue & Co, between 1844 and 1864.

107

French For Fun A New Instructive & Amusing Card Game. Pack of cards (60) with illustrations of objects and clothes in everyday use, published by John Jacques & Son Ltd, Kirby Street, London, EC1. Backs with Pierrot. With booklet of rules. In slip-case with pictorial label.
Lettered on the cards with captions in French, and on the label on the slip-case with title, publisher's name and address, etc.
Colour lithographs. Each 9.1 × 6.2cm (CR); in slip-case 9.7 × 7.1 cm.
E.1419.1-60—1986
Given by Mr CG Brookes

108

KNEPPER & CO, E. (1860)

Piquet cards (32), published by E Knepper & Co, Vienna, 3rd quarter of 19th century. Backs with a chequer pattern. In slip-case with King of Leaves on the front.
Lettered on the Seven of Bells with maker's name, and on the Deuce of Acorns and the Deuce of Hearts with maker's name and address.
Etchings and colour stencil. Each 9.1 × 5.5 cm; in case 9.4 × 6.1 cm.
E.1858.1-32—1885

109

Trappola cards (36), double-ended; the two Knaves of each suit depict Swiss heroes, and the Deuces of each suit depict the Four Seasons. Published by E Knepper & Co, Vienna, c.1860. Backs plaid pattern. In slip-case with the Deuce depicting summer on the front.
Lettered on the Seven of Acorns with maker's name and address, and on the Knave with titles. Stamped on the Knave of Hearts with date *1860* and maker's name. [Hargrave, p.264 (a similar set dated 1885]
Etchings and colour stencil. Each 9.3 × 5.7 cm.; in slip-case 9.9 × 6.3 cm
E.1829.1-36—1885

110

KRATOCHVIL, Antonis

Pack of cards (32), standard Bohemian pattern, published by Antonis Kratochvil, successor to M Severy of Prague, c.1860. Backs with zig-zag pattern.
Lettered on Deuce of Acorns *M Severy Nástupie Ant. Kratochvil, Praha* and on the Deuce of Hearts *v Praze*. Stamped on the Eight of Bells with Duty stamp *K.K.Kartenstempel 30* and maker's name etc.
Lithographs and colour stencil (?). Each 10.1 × 6 cm.
E.461.1-32—1973
Given by Mr AE Gunther

111

LENTHALL, John (worked early 1660s-c.1717)

Love cards, or The Intrigues and Amusements of that Passion merrily display'd. Pack of 52 cards, non-standard. On the Ace of Hearts is a caricature of Sir John Hewson, the regicide. The suit signs are on miniature cards on the top left and right-hand corners of the cards. Published by John Lenthall, c.1710. Backs plain. [O'Donoghue, No.71; Morley, pp.186,187]
Each lettered with captions and on the

Ace of Diamonds *Sold Only, at Willerton's Toy Shop, Bond Street.*
Engravings. Each 9.2 × 6.2 cm.
nos. 20368.1-52

See also S Mann, pp. 145 (Lenthall's advertisement No. XXIV)

112

Another pack, with two cards missing
E. 56.1-50—1971

See also ANONYMOUS: ENGLISH, 3rd quarter of 18th century, educational cards, sold at Willerton's Toy Shop, post 1760.
A pack entitled 'Delightful Cards', Lenthall, c. 1660-62 (Guildhall, No. 544), shows Hewson on the King of Hearts, holding a sword and a shoe, and has the caption: 'Hewson be skill amongst Knaves,/Knaves love his Company'. The Ace of Spades in this pack has a Charles II Duty stamp.

113

LEQUART,–(worked late 19th century)

Pack of 78 tarot cards, known as 'German Tarot', French suited, double-ended, the numerals with chinoiserie scenes and figures. Published by Lequart, Paris, c. 1895 [BN, 120; François, p. 177; Keller, FRA 401].
Backs with a black and white undulating pattern of chequers.
Lettered on the court cards with maker's name and address. Stamped on the Ace of Clubs *Republique Francaise Decret Du Avril 1890.*
Colour lithographs. Each 10.3 × 5.5 cm. (CR)
E. 1546.1-78—1926
Given by Mr A Myers Smith
See also GRIMAUD, BP

114

LITHOGRAFISKA AKTIEBOLAGET, NORRKÖPING

Pack of 52 cards, standard, Paris pattern, courts double-ended, published by Lithografiska Aktiebolaget, Norrköping, Sweden, 3rd quarter of 19th century. Backs with diagonal pattern of dots and swirls.

Lettered on court cards with titles, *Charles, Judith, Rachel,* etc. Stamped on the Duty Ace of Hearts with Duty stamp and *Lithografiska Aktiebolaget Norrköping.*
Colour lithographs. Each 8.9 × 6.1 cm.
E. 1837.1-52—1885

Another pack, identical, but the backs in blue instead of red.
E. 1869.1-52—1885

115

MACCHI, F (worked 1st half of 19th century)

Cards (32) from a fortune-telling pack, published by F Macchi, Prague, 1st half of 19th century. Backs plain green.
Lettered on the King of Hearts *F Macchi. Praha Platnyrska Ulice C 112.*
Each card lettered with titles in Czechslovakian and in German.
Woodcuts and colour stencil. Each 8.3 × 5 cm.
no. 29569.0.1-32

116

MACLURE, MACDONALD & MACGREGOR, (worked 3rd quarter of 19th century)

Pack of 52 transformation cards, published by Maclure, Macdonald & Macgregor, 77A Market Street, Manchester, c. 1865. Backs with diaper gold star on pink. [Keller, ENG 143 (back pattern colour variant); Mann p. 170]
Lettered on the Ace of Spades with maker's name and address etc and with mock Duty stamp design incorporating a caricature head of a woman.
Colour lithographs. Each 9.4 × 6.4 cm.
E. 5447.1-52—1960
Given by Mr CR Powter

Another pack with variant back pattern colour is listed in the *Catalogue of the Henry D Phillips Collection*, London, 1903, No. 258.

117

MAURIN & CIE, Charles (worked 3rd quarter of 19th century)

Pack of 52 piquet cards, Paris portraits, standard, double-ended, published by Charles Maurin & Cie, Paris, 3rd quarter of 19th century. Backs with bees in gold. With wrapper No.13 (Ancien Maison Arnoult), maker's trademark etc. and label No.8. With eagle watermark. Lettered on the court cards *Charles, Judith, Lahire* etc.
Colour lithographs. Each 8.1 × 5.2 cm (CR)
E.1831.1-52—1885

Another pack, with plain backs
E.1840.1-52—1885 (CR)

Another pack, with pink backs
E.1849.1-32—1885

Another pack, with pale orange backs
E.1856.1-52—1885

Another pack (32 cards). Seaweed pattern in maroon on backs.
E.1857.1-32—1885

Another pack (32 cards), with spot and diamond diaper in black on backs. With fragmentary wrapper, and complete wrapper No.6.
E.1862.1-32—1885 (CR)

Another pack (32 cards), with same back pattern in blue.
E.1865.1-32—1885 (CR)

Another pack (32 cards), plain backs.
E.1867.1-32—1885

Another pack (32 cards), same back pattern as E.1857
E.1868.1-32—1885

118

MONASTA, Antonino (worked late 17th century)

Cards (40), full length figures, Neapolitan pattern, published by Antonino Monasta, (?) Sicily, late 17th and early 18th century. Backs with flower and stem motif, within a rectangular border folded over to form a narrow border to the front of the cards. Lettered on the Four of Swords with maker's name, on the Ace of Money *Il Leon*, and on the Deuce of Swords *Con licenza del Re N.S.* The Six of Money is stamped with (?) *R.C.* and (?) a collector's mark.
Woodcuts, coloured by hand. Each 8.8 × 4.5 cm.
no.29285.1-40

The coat of arms on the Ace of Money is possibly that of Ferdinand and Isabella and the designs are Spanish, the Queen being replaced by the Knight. The inscriptions are however in Italian.

119

MÜLLER, HF (1809-1826), Copy after

Pack of 52 transformation cards, copies of those produced by HF Müller, Vienna, 1818-19. The Spade suit illustrates a Viennese story 'Beatrice'. With French suit signs. This pack was issued, a few at a time, in the *Repository of Arts*, 1818-19. [Hargrave, p.146] Stipple-engravings, coloured by hand. Each 9.2 × 6.5 cm.
E.513.1-52—1885

120

Pictorial Cards in Thirteen Plates, each containing Four Subjects, Partly Designed from the Subjoined Tale of Beatrice; or The Fracas, London, 1819.
28-page booklet, thread stitched, in paper covers, with four cards from the pack, pasted on the front.
E.513A—1885

121

MÜLLER, Johannes & Cie (1889-1940)

Pack of 36 cards, published by Johannes Müller & Cie, Schaffhausen & Basle, Switzerland, late 19th century. Backs with trailing stems and fleurettes. Lettered on the Deuce of Hearts *J Müller & Cie* and on the Deuce of Bells *Schaffhausen & Basle*.
Colour lithographs. Each 8.7 × 5.4 cm (CR)
E.459.1-36—1973
Given by Mr AE Gunther

The address of the Müller firm was abbreviated to 'Schaffhausen' between 1940 and 1960. From 1960 the name was changed to A.G. Müller & Cie.

122

Pack of 78 tarot cards, produced by Johannes Müller & Cie, Schaffhausen c.1914. Backs brown and green diagonal plaid. [Keller, SWI 16 (dated 1885)]
Lettered on the Deuce of Money *Fabrique De Cartes A Schaffhouse* (sic), and on the Four of Money *JR* (monogram).
Colour lithographs. Each 11 × 6.2 cm (CR)
E.501-578—1934
Given by Major CC Adams, M.C., F.S.A.

123

'NEDERLAND' SPEELKAARTENFABRIEK

Cards (52, and Joker) of a standard, double-ended pack, the Aces with Dutch topographical scenes. Published by the 'Nederland' Speelkaartenfabriek, Amsterdam, 2nd quarter of 20th century. Backs with panel of red cubes. [Keller, HOL 6]
Lettered on the Aces with place names and on the Joker *The Jolly Joker*.
Colour lithographs. Each 9.1 × 6.1 cm (CR)
E.1435-1487—1934

124

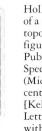

Hollandia Whist. Cards (52, and Joker) of a double-ended pack, the Aces with topographical scenes, the courts with figures in national costumes. Published by the 'Nederland' Speelkaartenfabriek, Amsterdam (Middelburg), 2nd quarter of 20th century. Backs with Dutch tiles. [Keller, HOL 38]
Lettered on the Aces and on the courts with place names, and on the Joker (a boy fishing from a jetty) *The Jolly Joker*.
Colour lithographs. Each 9.1 × 6.2 cm (CR)
E.1488-1540—1934

125

NEJEDLY, Johann (worked 2nd half of 19th century)

Pack of 36 cards, double-ended, published by Johann Nejedly, Vienna, 2nd half of 19th century. Backs with zig-zag.
Lettered on the Ten of Money *Joh.Nejedly Wien*, on the Ace of Batons *Joh: Nejedly. Erfinder und Privil.Besitzer*, and on the Deuce of Swords *Neu Erfundene K.K.Aus.Priv.Wasch Karten Fabricirt In Wien*.
Woodcuts and colour stencil. Each 12.6 × 6 cm.
E.1834.1-36—1885

126

Pack of 54 tarocco cards, double-ended, French suits, published by Johann Nejedly, Vienna, late 19th century. Backs with zig-zag. [Not in Kaplan]
Lettered on the Knave of Clubs *Niederlage ob:Bräunerst. No.1135 Von Joh: Nejedly in Wien Fabrik in Otta Kring Langegasse No.245*, on the Knave of Diamonds *Spiel-Karten Kaiserl:Königl: aus privilegirten* and on the Numeral II *Johann Nejedly*. Stamped on the Ace of Hearts with the Imperial eagle and *No.41 Joh.Nejedly In Wien*.
Etchings and colour stencil. Each 10.9 × 5.4 cm (CR)
E.6299.1-54—1910

127

NEUMAYER, J (worked c.1890)

Tarot cards (52, from a pack of 54), double-ended, the numerals with rural scenes and figures, published by F Piatnik & Sons, Vienna, late 19th century. From a series entitled 'Industrie und Gluck' (Industry and Fortune) [BN, No.102] Backs with diagonal plaid. Fragmentary wrapper No.36.
Lettered on the Knave of Clubs (twice) *Ferd. Piatnik & Söhne. Wien.XIV, Hütteldorferstrasse 229-231*, on the Hordeman of Clubs *J Neumayer*, on the Knave of Diamonds *Ferd. Piatnik & Söhne, Wien 89*, on the Ace of Hearts *Schutzmarke* (horse and jockey) *Ferd. Piatnik & Söhne, Wien 1598*, and on a blank card again with maker's name.
Colour lithographs. Each 11.3 × 6.3 cm.
E.30.1-52—1951
Given by Mr Godfrey Lias

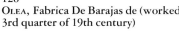

128
OLEA, Fabrica De Barajas de (worked 3rd quarter of 19th century)

Pack of 48 cards, standard, published by Fabrica de Barajas de Olea, Cadiz, Spain. Backs with interlacing in pink and blue. Lettered on the Four of Money *Fabrica De Barajas De Olea Premiado Calle De Las Flores N-1 Cadiz*; on the Deuce of Money *1er Superfino*; on the Four of Cups *Olea, Cadiz*; on the Deuce of Cups *Naipes Deunaoja Primer Florete*; on the Six of Swords *Viteladehilo*; on the Seven of Money *Del No.5*; on the Five of Batons *Anode 1866*, and on the Ace of Swords *Cortetabla*.
Colour lithographs. Each 9.1 × 6.1 cm.
E.1859.1-48—1885
Given by Senor José Joaquin de Carreras

129
OTH, Clas (worked c.1507-c.1565), In the style of

Five cards. (?)Nuremberg, early or mid-16th century.
Woodcuts, four coloured by hand. Each 7.3 × 4.8 cm.
E.989-993—1920
Purchased under the Bequest of Capt. HB Murray, ex coll. Major Henry Harvard.
For other cards by Clas Oth, see *Nuremberg: Germanisches Museum. Katalog der Kartenspiele und Spielkarten*, Nos.71-169,256-287, with plates. Rosenfeld dates the cards, known as the Stukely cards, which resemble the above, between 1546-1550 [Rosenfeld, p.19].

The Knave of Bells
E.989—1920

The Five of Acorns
E.990—1920

The Knave of Acorns
E.991—1920

Four of Leaves
E.992—1920

Eight of Leaves
E.993—1920

130
OTTLEY, William Young (1771-1836)

Cards (47, from a pack of 52), with Italian suits, but with the Money suit signs represented by pomegranates [Bartsch, Vol. VI, 2, 1-34, 40-42; Morley, pp.70-71; Hargrave, p.95].
Copies by WY Ottley published in *A Collection of Fac-Similes of Scarce and Curious Prints . . .*, London, 1828, Nos.43-89.
Engravings. Cut to average size 13.5 × 7.5 cm.
Nos.13891.47-93

The original set, from which there are

five missing cards, has been variously attributed to Israel van Maecken or to Martin Schoengauer, or to the Bavarian monogrammist MZ, or alternatively to Nikolaus Mair of Landshut. See *Schweizer Spielkarten*, Kunstgewerbe Museum, Zurich, 1979.

Other impressions (6)
nos.29741.A.51,53,68,69,117,244.

131
THE MASTER P W OF COLOGNE

The Nine of Rabbits (or Hares).
Lettered in Arabic and in Roman numerals 9 and *VIIII*.
Engraving. Circular, cut to 6.3 cm.
E.14—1923

From a set published c.1470, in which the suits are animals and flowers. The complete set consists of thirteen cards – Rabbits (or Hares), Pinks, Columbines, Parrots and Roses.
This card has been trimmed; the uncut state has a border of three lines.
Copies of the set were issued c.1500 by Telman von Wesel.
See Max Lehrs, *Geschichte und Kritischer Katalog des Deutschen, Niederländischen und Französischen Kupferstichs im XV Jahrhundert*, Vol.VII, Vienna, 1930, p.295,V.

132
PANICHI, GIO

Cards (48, from a pack of 52), full length figures. The backs with engraved figures of halberdiers in 17th century costume, holding shields with the Medici arms. Florence, late 18th or early 19th century (?).
Lettered within the material, on the Six of Hearts *G.I.O. Panichi*, and with (?) the weaver's mark.
Engraving and woven silk. Each 9.5 × 5.5 cm.
E.6296.1-48—1910

'. . . embroidered (*sic*) silk cards have been exhibited at Kensington'. (Willshire, p.28)

133
PARIS, Abbé (worked late 18th century)

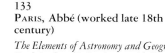

The Elements of Astronomy and Geography Explained on 40 Cards, beautifully Engraved and Coloured By the Abbé Paris. Published by John Wallis, 16 Ludgate Street, London, 1795. [Keller, ENG 116; Hargrave, p.210, 211] Backs with letterpress information. In marbled paper slip-case, with engraved pictorial title label.
Lettered on the title label with title etc. and *Published July 15th.1795*.

Engravings, coloured by hand. Each 9.1 × 6.2 cm.; in slip-case 9.4 × 6.5 cm.
E.820.1-41—1939
Given by Mr Robert Cust

134
PIATNIK, Ferdinand & Sons (1824-part 1967)

Cards (36, from a pack of 52), standard, full length figures, published by F Piatnik & Sons, Vienna, c.1900. [Keller, AUS 61] Backs with black on red zig-zag.
Lettered on the Seven of Hearts *Ferd. Piatnik & Söhne. Wien. XIII. Hütteldorferstr. 205*, on the Eight of Hearts *Niederlage Stadt Freisingergasse No 6*, on the Eight of Bells *Ferd. Piatnik & Söhne. Wien. Registrierte Schutzmarke*, and on the Six of Bells *Weli*. The Eight of Bells stamped *K.K.Kartenstempel 14*. Lineblock and colour stencil. Each 9.8 × 5.5 cm.
E.510.1-36—1951
Given by Mr W Robinow

Cards (52 from a pack of 54), in the 'Industrie und Glück' series of tarot cards, produced by F Piatnik & Sons, Vienna, c.1890. See NEUMEYER, J.

135
RAUME (or RAUNE)

Sheet of miniature cards (36), standard Bavarian pattern c.1840. [Keller, GER sheet 226; Bierdimpfle 80]
Lettered on the Six of Hearts *Raume* (?).
Etching. 10.2 × 8.5 cm.
E.591A—1885
Given by the Bavarian National Museum

136
REED, Edward Tennyson (1860-1933)

Panko or Votes for Women. The Great Card Game. Suffragists v. Anti-Suffragists. Cards (48), comprising a set divided into 8 series of 6 cards each, numbered 10, 20, 30 and 40, with illustrations satirizing the Suffragist Movement, some bearing caricatures of political figures of the day. In slip-case with letterpress label on the front and an impression of one of the cards on the back. Published by Peter Gurney Ltd, c.1912-18. Backs with formal floral and interlace.
Each card signed with monogram *ETR* and lettered with a catch-phrase. The label on the slip-case lettered with title and *Pictures by ET Reed, of Punch*. Peter Gurney, Ltd., 2 Breams Buildings, London, E.C. Copyright.
Colour offset. Each 8.9 × 6 cm.; in case 9.5 × 7 cm.
E.625.1-48—1972
Given by Mr I Gray

Cards bearing political caricatures are:
4	Turn 'Em Out	David Lloyd George
6	" " "	Arthur James Balfour
5	" " "	Austen Chamberlain
3	" " "	Herbert Henry Asquith
2	" " "	Winston Churchill
Pank! Pank! Pank!		Mrs Pankhurst
Fourteen Days		Lord Lansdowne

137
REYNOLDS, Joseph

Pack of 52 cards, standard, full length figures, published by Joseph Reynolds, between 1806 and 1820. Backs plain. In slip-case with blue lining.
Lettered on the Duty Ace of Spades *G.III.Rex. Duty One Shilling And Sixpence. Josh. Reynolds.*
Woodcuts and colour stencil, the Ace of Spades engraved. Each 9.3 × 6.4 cm.
E.2911.1-52—1948
Given by Mrs EM Halsey

Hargrave refers to a transformation pack by this maker, whom she mistakenly names 'Joseph H. Reynolds'. Otherwise he appears to be unknown.

138
REYNOLDS & SONS

Pack of 52 cards, standard, courts full length, published by Reynolds & Sons, between 1850-62. Backs with diaper fleurettes.
Lettered on the Ace of Spades with maker's name and *Duty One Shilling*.
Woodcuts, printed in blue, and colour stencil, the Ace of Spades engraved. Each 9.3 × 6.5 cm (CR)
E.2582.1-52—1917
Given by Mr Arthur Myers Smith

139

Duty stamp. 1803. (Ace of Spades)
Lettered *G.III Rex. Josh. Reynolds,
Exportation*. Numbered *13*.
Engraving. Cut to 8.5 × 6.2 cm.
E.852—1950
Given by Mrs IW Bailey

140

ROSSETTI, Dante Gabriel (1828-1882)

Designs for playing cards (5). The King
of Spades (a skeleton as a sexton grave-
digging); the King of Hearts (a bust of
Shakespeare); the Queen of Hearts (a
sovereign coin with a profile of Queen
Victoria); the King of Diamonds (a
caricature of Louis Philippe), and the
King of Clubs (Mr Punch and dog Toby
holding a scroll). 1847. Unpublished.
Lettered with titles and E.152 *The
Reigning Sovereign 1845* etc, E.154
Instituted For The Suppression Of Humbug.
Lithographs. Sheet
E.150-154—1928
Given by Mrs Moeller

141

ROWLEY & CO

Pack of 52 cards, non-standard, the
courts portraits of the Kings and Queens
of England, France, Spain and Russia,
and the suits Cups, Clover leaves,
Diamonds and Spearheads. Published by
Rowley & Co, between 1774 and 1776.
Backs plain. [Willshire, E.169
(numbered *10*); Morley, p.159-161;
Hargrave, p.204,205 (numbered *17*);
Hoffmann, pl.]
Lettered on the Ace of Spearheads
G.III.Rex Rowley & Co. Numbered *2*.
Engravings, printed in blue, red and
green. Each 9.2 × 6.3 cm (CR)
nos.29336.1-52

Another pack. Numbered *8*
E.2153-2204—1920

Another pack. Numbered *11*
E.2910.1-52—1948
Given by Mrs EM Halsey

142

**S, G (? Giles SAVOURÉ) (worked
c.1480-c.1506)**

Sheet of playing cards (6), consisting of
two complete impressions and one cut
impression each of the Knave of
Diamonds and the Knave of Hearts.
Lyons, late 15th century.
Signed on the Knave of Hearts *G:Cartier*
and on the Knave of Diamonds *G.S*.
Woodcuts, coloured by hand. Size of
sheet 19.4 × 13.2 cm.
E.988—1920

Repr. J Seguin, *Le Jeu de Carte*, Paris,
1968, p.57 (col.); Seguin states that the
sheet is probably of Lyonnais
workmanship and is to be dated to the
late 15th century. H-R D'Allemagne,
Les Cartes a Jouer . . ., Paris, 1906,
Vol.2, p.622, lists Giles Savouré,
working at Lyons c.1480-c.1506.

This sheet has been preserved in a 16th
century binding to *Le Trésor de l'Ame*,
published by L Cruse, Geneva, 1494.

Purchased under the Bequest of Capt.
HB Murray, ex coll. Major Henry
Harvard

143

**SCARFE, Gerald (born 1926), and
other artists**

Playing Politics or Cabinet Shuffle. Pack
of 52 cards, and two Jokers, published
by the Victoria and Albert Museum, in
association with InterCol. London,
1983. Courts, Aces and Jokers have
caricature portraits by Gerald Scarfe and
other cartoonists of the Prime Minister,
Ministers of State and members of the
four main political parties. Backs with
Tudor portcullis. In similarly decorated
slip-case, with reproduction of one of the
Jokers on the front, and an explanatory
leaflet by Yasha Beresiner and Nicky
Bird, giving a short history of politico-
historical cards, and biographies of the
artists.
Colour screenprints. Each 8.9 × 6.4 cm
(CR); in slip-case 9.3 × 7.3 cm.
E.1450.1-55—1983

Given by the Department of Museum
Services, V & A Museum

The other artists are:
John Springs (born 1960)
Marc (Marc Boxer) (born 1931)
Trog (Wally Fawkes) (born 1924)

SEVERY, M See KRATOCHVIL, Antonis

144

SIMON, F (worked early 20th century)

See also GRIMAUD, Baptiste-Paul

Hollandaises Illustrées. Pack of 52 cards for Whist, non-standard, courts double-ended figures in 16th century costume, published by BP Grimaud, Paris, c.1910. [Keller, FRA 370, red] Backs with butterfly and stems of flowers in blue.
Lettered on the courts *BP Grimaud Paris*.
Stamped on the Ace of Clubs with blue Duty stamp of the Republic (1890).
Colour lithographs. Each 9.2 × 6.4 cm (CR)
E.1120-1171—1934

145

Pack of 52 cards, similar pattern to above, plus Joker and blank card, published by BP Grimaud, Paris, c.1915. [Keller, FRA 367] Backs with blue circle and squares.
Lettered on court cards and on Joker *B.P. Grimaud France* and *B.P. Grimaud Paris* respectively. Stamped on Ace of Clubs with blue Duty stamp of the Republic (1890).
Colour lithographs. Each 8.5 × 5.6 cm (CR)
E.1066-1119—1934

146

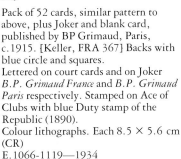

SMITH, Pamela Colman (1877/78-c.1950)

Pack of 78 cartomantic tarots, published by Arthur Edward Waite, London, 1916. Backs with mosaic. [Keller, ENG 37, 38 (c.1920; c.1937); Kaplan 272; Dummett, pl.32, p.154 et seq; BN: 149 (re-edition by A.G.Müller & Cie, 1972)]
Each signed with artist's monogram *PCS*.
Colour lithographs. Each 11.9 × 7 cm.
E.423-500—1934
Given by Major CC Adams

The first edition of the game appeared in 1910, illustrating Waite's *The Key to the Tarot*.

147

SOLESIO, Felix & Sons, (worked late 18th century), Possibly by

Pearwood printing block, cut on both sides, and a sheet of cards printed from one side. Possibly by Felix Solesio & Sons, Madrid, late 18th century.
Lettered on the Five of Swords *Carte Fine*, on the Ace of Coins with arms of Spain and *Carlus Deigrazia Hispania* etc.
Size of block, approx 40.5 × 26.5 × 4 cm.
no.322—1885

148

SOLIS, Virgil (1514-1562)

Three cards from a pack of 52. (?) c.1544.

Five of Monkies: Lettered *V*.
No.12841.2

Five of Peacocks: Lettered *V*.
No.12841.4

One of Parrots: signed with monogram *VS*. Lettered *I* and *Rot*. No.12841.3

Engravings. Cut to 9.1 × 6 cm.; 9.4 × 6 cm.; 9.3 × 6.1 cm.

See Ilse O'Dell-Franke, *Kupferstiche und Radierungen aus der Werkstatt des Virgil Solis*, Wiesbaden, 1977

149

TOWNROE, Reuben (1835-1911)

Cards (16) from a pack of 52, being the three courts and the Ace for each of the four suits, with portraits of European royalties and the Presidents of Switzerland and of the USA, also of John Brown, Queen Victoria's servant.
Published by De La Rue & Co, London, 1874. Backs plain red.
Lettered with names of countries.
Colour lithographs. Each 9.3 × 6.5 cm.
Sir Henry Cole Bequest

Sir Henry Cole on p.103 of his *Fifty Years of Public Work*, Vol.1, London, 1884, states that 'my last attempt in Art Manufactures was the production in 1874 of a set of international playing cards, designed by Mr Townroe, and published by Messrs Thomas de la Rue'.
The pack described by Willshire [p.232, 233, E.173] has backs with the Royal Arms of England, with those of Saxe-Coburg-Gotha, on a shield of pretence, printed in gold on a blue background.

Four examples in various colours of the decorated backs are in the Henry Cole Bequest.

153

VIASSONE, Alessandro (born 1830)

Pack of 78 Piedmontese tarots, published by Alessandro Viassone, Turin, 1932. [Keller, ITA 40 (similar)] Backs with diagonal check in black and green.
Lettered on Ace of Money *Alessandro Viassone Torino Via Cabotto Corso Re Umberto 100-102*. Dated *Mar. 1932*.
Colour lithographs. Each 10.6 × 6.1 cm (CR)
E.735-812—1934
Given by Major CC Adams, M.C., F.S.A.

150

The UNITED STATES PLAYING CARD Co (worked 20th century)

Little Duke Toy Cards No.24. Pack of 52 miniature cards, French suits, courts double-ended, published by the United States Playing Card Co, Cincinnati, USA, c.1929. [Keller, USA 159] Backs with conventional formalized leaf pattern and central medallion. In slip-case.
Lettered on Ace of Spades with title, name and address of maker, trademark, etc.
Colour lithographs. Each 4.4 × 3.1 cm.
E.794.1-52—1950
Given by Mr H Barkley

154

Pack of 40 hombre cards, from a standard pack of 52, published by Alessandro Viassone, Turin, 1932. Backs with black diagonal check.
Lettered on Ace of Hearts *A. Viassone Torino* and with Duty stamp, and dated *Ott.1932*. Lettered on each of courts *A Viassone Torino*.
Colour lithographs. Each 8.9 × 5.7 cm (CR)
E.1026-1065—1934
Given by Major CC Adams, M.C., F.S.A.

151

Hornet 6. Pack of 52 cards, standard, courts double-ended, published by the US Playing Card Co, Windsor, Ontario, Canada, 2nd quarter of 20th century. Backs with eight dolphins, in red.
Lettered on Ace of Spades with title, maker's name and address, and on two additional cards *Made in Canada*, and with guarantee, rules etc respectively.
Colour line blocks. Each 8.7 × 6.2 cm (CR)
E.866-919—1934
Given by Major CC Adams, M.C., F.S.A.

152

VALLANCE, Aymer (1862-1943)

Pack of 52 cards, courts double-ended and with pseudo-French figures, published by the Peerless Playing Card Company, London, c.1900. Backs with stylized flower and leaf design in blue and gold.
Lettered on Ace of Spades with maker's name, and on courts in archaic lettering.
Colour letterpress. Each 9.1 × 6.5 cm (CR)
E.256.1-52—1953
Given by Miss LMC Jones

155

VISENTINI (VICENTINI), Antonio (1688-1782)

Pack of 52 biblical cards, the suits being Discs (yellow), Diamonds (pink), Hearts (lavender) and Jars (buff); each card illustrates an episode from the Old Testament and bears within the suit sign an emblem whose significance is explained in the text below the illustration. The cards are unnumbered but each is lettered with capital or lower-case letters. Etched by A Visentini after designs by Francesco Zuccarelli, 1748. [Keller, ITA 114; Hargrave, p.242; Berry, 34] Backs speckled. In contemporary slip-case of stamped leather, lined with floral decorative paper.
Signed on the Y of Jars *A Visentini*.

Lettered *F.Z.I.1748*. Each card lettered with descriptive text in Italian and most with 2 lines of Italian and 2 lines of Latin verse.
Etchings, coloured by hand. Each 10 × 5.7 cm.; in slip-case 11.1 × 6 × 2.9 cm.
E.449—1953

An incomplete pack of 33 cards is E.6302.1-33—1910. There is another incomplete pack of 33 cards in the Guildhall Collection (No.26).

156
VOLAY, Jehan (worked c.1568-c.1571), or GOYRAND, Jean (worked c.1480-c.1500)

Sheet of cards, possibly produced by Jehan Volay or by Jean Goyrand, both of Lyons. Modern impression.
Lettered on one of the Knaves *IC* (?), and on the central band *IG IC* (?).
Lettered on the Queen card *Vive.Les. Bons.Enfans. Qui. Iovent. Sowent.*
Woodcut. 38.7 × 31.7 cm.
No.16296 (E.705—1913)

157
VOYSEY, Charles Francis Annersley (1857-1941)

Design for a card back, a double-ended image of a King, a Knave and two Queens.
Watercolour and pen. 9 × 6.4 cm.
E.297—1913

Repr. Frances Hicklin, *Playing Cards*, V & A Small Colour Book No.12, HMSO, 1976, pl.9.

158
WADDINGTON LTD, John

Pack of 52 cards advertising 'Fairy' dyes on the backs, published by John Waddington Ltd, London and Leeds, c.1900-1925.
Lettered on Ace of Spades with maker's name and registration number *704615*.
Half-tone blocks, printed in green. Each 5.9 × 9 cm.
Circ. 19.1-52—1976

159
Pack of 52 cards and a Joker, advertising 'Old Castle' Scotch whiskey, published by John Waddington Ltd, London and Leeds, c.1900-1925.
Lettered on Ace of Spades with maker's name and registration number *704615*.
Half-tone blocks, printed in green. Each 5.9 × 9 cm.
Circ. 20.1-53—1976

Exhib. 'The Objects of Advertising', Department of Circulation, V & A Museum, 1976.

160
Packs (2) each of 52 cards, the backs decorated with aircraft, 'Supermarine S 6' and 'Vickers Victoria', published by John Waddington Ltd.
Colour offset. Each 8.9 × 5.8 cm (CR); in box 6.4 × 19.2 cm.
E1422a.(46)—1986, E1422b.(38)—1986
Given by Mr CG Brooks

161
WEIGEL, JC (1654-1725)

Cards (36), showing men and women in occupational costumes of Augsburg, published by JC Weigel, Augsburg, post 1720. Backs plain. [Hoffmann, F No.123, similar pack; O'Donoghue, Nos.356, 357, similar packs]
Lettered in German and in French with titles.
Engravings, coloured by hand. Each 9.6 × 5.3 cm.; in case 10.5 × 6 cm.
E.4789.1-36—1960
Given by Mr MT Colchester

Some of the figures are derived from a series of 21 plates of costumes of Augsburg, published by Jeremias Wolff (1664-1724), of Augsburg, 1720.

162
WHEELER, T (worked early 19th century)

Duty stamp. 1803 (Ace of Spades)
Lettered *G.III Rex. T. Wheeler.*
Numbered 69 etc.
Engravings. Cut to 10 × 6.3 cm.
E.850—1950
Given by Mrs IW Bailey

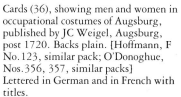

VII

WAGEN

163

WONSCHICK, Helmut (born 1947)

Bilder Zum tarot. Pack of 24 cards (including a title-card and a card with descriptive details), illustrating the Major Arcana of the tarot pack, published by the artist, Berlin, 1984. The backs with an empty frame with ribbon mouldings. In slip-case with the design of the title-card on the front, and the card with descriptive details on the back.
Signed and dated in ink on the slip-case *H. Wonschick 21.XII.84* and inscribed *Sample Copy to Victoria u. Albert Museum from the Artist*. Each card lettered with artist's copyright. The title-card and numeral IV (Herrscher) signed and dated *H W 84* and *H W 1984* respectively. Lettered on the card with descriptive details *Die Zauberin, die zur Hohepriesterin . . . Spiegel zu schauen.* Numbered 0 *to* XXI.
Offset lithography. Each 13 × 8 cm.; in slip-case 13.2 × 8.1 cm (CR)
E.2.1-25—1985
Given by the artist

A series of pen and ink drawings, each measuring 30 × 20 cm. were made by the artist for this pack. It is the artist's third tarot.

164

Cards (4), Jokers, from a pack of cards for Rommé (Rummy). 1984.
E.11 lettered *Fou*; E.12 lettered *Joker*; E.13 lettered *Fool* and E.14 signed with monogram and dated *HW 81*. Each card signed and dated on the back *H W* and *Wonschick 84*. Inscribed *Müster* (patterns).
Screenprints, coloured by hand. Each 9 × 6 cm (CR)
E.11-14—1985
Given by the artist

165

Sheet with a deck of cards (56), including Jokers (4), also the design for the backs, for the game of Rommé (Rummy). 1982. The frame incorporates a drawing of grotesques in a landscape. Signed in pencil and dated *Wonschick 82*. Inscribed *To the collection of the Victoria and Albert Museum.* Numbered *100/200 Siebdruck* (screenprint).
Screenprint. 56.5 × 83.5 cm.
E.15—1985
Given by the artist

Ninety-nine additional decks were printed and hand-coloured by the artist. This was the artist's second deck of cards.

166

Sheet with a deck of cards (32) for a game entitled 'Skatspiel'. 1980. Signed in pencil and dated *Wonschick 1980*. Inscribed *Müster* (patterns).
Screenprint. 35.1 × 48.1 cm.
E.16—1985
Given by the artist

The game of 'Skat' originated in the Harz Mountains between 1810-20, and is derived from an ancient game entitled 'Schafkopf' (Sheepshead). This was the artist's first deck of cards. See 'Helmut Wonschick', Galerie Gey, Hagen, 9 March to 15 April 1981, Cat. nos. 15-20.

167

WÜST, CL (1811-post 1900)

Miniature packs (2) of 52 cards each, produced by CL Wüst, Frankfurt-on-Main, third quarter of 19th century. French suits, double-ended. Backs plain pink and green respectively. [Keller, GER 135 (backs differ)] In slip-case of decorative papers. Each lettered on the Four of Hearts with manufacturer's name and address.
Colour lithographs. Each 1.7 × 1.2 cm.
E.1548, 1549—1926 (For illustration see colour plate page 21)
Given by A Myers Smith

These two packs are similar to the Dondorf pack [DH & MD, pp.68, 69].

Another pack, but with the King of Clubs missing. Backs, plain pink.

ANONYMOUS SECTION

CHINESE
168

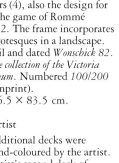

Cards (81) from a pack of 105 domino cards. Chinese, late 19th century. [Hargrave, p.10, illust.]
Colour lithographs. Each 8.6 × 1.9 cm.
E.463.1-81—1973
Given by Mr AE Gunther

The coins, scrolls and symbols are emblematic of the blessings of life.

169

Cards (36, from a pack of 52) depicting the Spanish Armada, from the Papal Council to the subsequent hanging of the Jesuits, published c.1680, as a protest against the leanings towards the Church of Rome, shown by the Duke of York, afterwards James II. Backs, geometrical pattern (see also 'The Popish Plot' by Francis BARLOW, nos.20366.1-52) [Willshire, E.185; Guildhall No.432]
Lettered with captions and numerals.
Engravings. Each 9 × 5.5 cm.
E.1184-1219—1921

Mann, pp.134,135, lists pack No.III advertised by John Lenthall 'At the Talbot against St. Dunstan's Church in Fleet-street London', not later than 1717, under the title of 'Navigational Cards', which depict the naval battles of the English and Spanish in Elizabeth's reign, which she equates with the 'Spanish Armada' pack. [See also Keller, ENG 108]

Other publishers of this or similar packs were Jonathan Wilkins & Jacob Sampson, also Robert Walton at the Globe, St Paul's Church Yard, c.1679. Several versions of the pack exist.

170

Marlborough's Victories [Willshire, E.192, 193; Keller, ENG 86] Pack of 52 politico-historical cards depicting the Duke of Marlborough's victories from 1702-1706, and various political incidents in the same period, with portraits of Queen Anne, etc c.1708. Backs plain.
Lettered with captions and numerals.
Engravings. Each 9.2 × 6 cm.
E.1238-1289—1921

171

Cards (31, from a pack of 52). Backs plain. First half of 18th century. Stamped on the Duty Ace of Spades with Duty Stamp and VI Pence, monogram AR or GR.
Woodcuts and colour stencil. Each 8.5 × 5.8 cm.
E.1720.1-31—1929
Given by the Misses Isabel and Margaret Basnett

The monogram on the Duty stamp cannot be identified clearly, but it is either AR or GR. The sixpenny duty was imposed under Queen Anne and under the Georges [see Hargrave, pp.182-185].

172

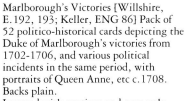

Cards (50, from a pack of 52 educational cards), the Ace of Diamonds and the Ace of Clubs are missing. [Hargrave, p.211; Mann, p.161] The rulers of England are depicted on the Hearts, Diamonds and Clubs suits, and on the courts of the Spades suit; the numerals of this suit carry tables of multiplication, measurements, etc. Each card has a miniature card with the suits in one corner. c.1760-70.
Lettered with names, dates, etc and on the Nine of Spades Sold at Willerton's Toy Shop Bond Street.
Engravings, coloured by hand. Each 9.4 × 6.2 cm.
nos.26546.1-50

Willerton's Toy Shop was in existence from the early 18th century until at least 1802, though R Willerton is only recorded in the rate book from 1769 onwards. See also John Lenthall, early 18th century, nos. 20368.1-52 and E.56—1971

173

Another pack, of 50 cards
E.641.1-50—1969

174

A Systematical Compendium of Geography. Pack of 52 cards and one card of instructions, with suit marks in the top left-hand corner only, the rest of the card being printed with geographical details of various countries in the four continents. 1790. [Morley, pp.133-135, instruction card differs; Mann, pp.125,126; Keller, ENG 90] In slip-case covered with a seaweed pattern paper. Backs plain.
Dated on the instructions card February 1790.
Colour woodcuts and letterpress. Each 9.4 × 6.3 cm (CR)
E.821.1-52—1939
Given by Mr Robert Cust

175

The Knave of Spades. c.1800. Plain back.
Woodcut and colour stencil. 9.2 × 6.3 cm (CR)
E.37—1935
Given by Mr F Marchant

176

Cards (45, from a pack of 52, including
2 Sevens of Clubs). c.1810.
In box E.403—1946
Woodcut and colour stencil, the Ace of
Spades engraved. Each 9.2 × 6.3 cm.
E.402.1-45—1946

177

Box for playing cards and counters,
decorated in the pseudo-Japanese style,
and containing mother-of-pearl card
counters of various designs, some
engraved with the monogram of
William Pringle, great-grandfather of
the donor. c.1810.
Box, lacquered in black and gold. 17.5
× 31.8 × 6.4 cm.
E.406—1946
Given by Mr AW Pringle

178

Transformation cards (13, from two
packs). c.1825. Backs plain pink.
E.303, 304, 311 inscribed respectively
*Punch; Clown; The Rivals; Baron de Crac a
frenchman of ye old School.*
Colour woodcuts, pen and ink and
watercolour. Each 9.2 × 6.4 cm.
E.299-311—1947
Given by Col. FP Roe

179

Cards (60) from several miniature packs,
standard, courts double-ended, with
arabic numerals in the suits. Late 19th
century. Backs plain, blue and pink.
Colour line blocks. Each 6.4 × 4.1 cm.
E.2904.1-60—1948
Given by Miss JC Arnold

180

Cards (2, of identical design) from a pack
advertising CWS biscuits made by the
Co-operative Wholesale Society,
Crumpsall Works, Manchester, c.1925.
Colour lithographs. Each 8.9 × 6.4 cm.
E.2304, 2305—1983
Given by Mr MJ Franklin

181

Card made of mother-of-pearl, with
coloured inlay. Paris pattern.
Lettered *David.*
7.8 × 5.5 cm.
E.6297—1910

182

Tarot cards (30) from a pack of the
Marseilles pattern with Italian suit
signs. French, probably mid 18th
century. Backs with a trellis with suns in
blue, pasted on, overlapping fronts.
Lettered with titles in French, Roman
numerals.
Woodcuts and colour stencil. Each 10.8
× 5.7 cm.
E.6306.1-30—1910

The back pattern is the same as that
described by Keller, FRA 163, which
was designed by Pierre Isnard and
published by Nicolas François Laudier,
1746.

183

The Pallas of Spades. Full length figure,
holding tulip, left profile, medallion
with Fleur-de-Lys on robe. Probably
third quarter of 18th century. Back
plain, used as an invitation card.
Lettered *Pallas.* Inscribed in ink on the
back *Monsieur Holgate est prié de la part de
Monsr. Thornton & de Mr & Madame
Godeffroy de souper chès eux Jeudi le 2e.
Avril R.s.v.p.*
Woodcut, and colour stencil. 8.7 ×
5.9 cm.
E.922—1933

184

Transformation cards (45, from a pack of 52), and two unfinished drawings for the Ten of Spades. The courts represent characters from literature, including *Le Barbier de Séville* by Caron de Beaumarchais. c.1830. Backs plain. The courts inscribed with titles and *R, V, D* respectively.
Pen lithographs, coloured by hand.
E.834.21, 22 pencil, pen and ink.
Each 11.8 × 8.3 cm.
E.834.1-47—1969
Given by Miss Annie Hall

185

Pack of 32 piquet cards, non-standard, full length figures of Justice, Liberté, Egalité, Humanité, Union, Force, Courage, Esperance, Jesus, Gracchus, Brutus and Lycurgue. Published in Paris, 1830 or 1848. Backs marbled in red.
[Hoffmann, 54a; Keller, FRA 330]
Lettered on the figure cards with titles etc.
Etchings, coloured by hand. Each 8 × 5.4 cm.
E.6295.1-32—1910

186

Pack of 52 cards, Paris portraits, standard, double-ended, 3rd quarter of 19th century. [Keller, FRA 25, 29, 30, 34 similar]
Lettered with titles *David, Pallas* etc and on the Knave of Clubs with the *1853 Administ. Des Contrib. Indir Gatteaux*, within a shield.
Colour lithographs. Each 8.4 × 5.3 cm (CR)
E.1547.1-52—1926
Given by Mr Arthur Myers Smith

With laurel wreath watermark 'C.I.' (Contributions Indirectes), which was introduced in 1875.

187

Piquet cards (29, from a pack of 32), the numerals transformations.
Probably French, c.1870. Backs, diaper spot and circle in red.
Colour lithographs and pen and ink.
Each 8.8 × 5.8 cm.
E.464.1-29—1973
Given by Mr AE Gunther

188

Transformation pack of 32 piquet cards, the courts of the Hearts and Diamonds suits are figures with animal heads.
Published in Paris, 1873.
Backs, diagonal plaid pattern.
[Hargrave, p.80; Mann, pp.170, 171]
Lettered on the courts *Roi; Dame; Valet.*
Colour lithographs. Each 9.2 × 6.4 cm.
E.458.1-32—1973
Given by Mr AE Gunther

GERMAN

189

Cards (16). 1750. (G.1026-1041)
Bierdimpfle Nos.24 & 65)
Lettered on the Deuce of Acorns *Sigl Ambt München* and on the King of Hearts *Churfüstl. Karten.*
Woodcuts. Each 9.3 × 7 cm.
E.581.1-16—1885

190

Cards (16). [G.1042-1057; Bierdimpfle Nos.23 & 64]
Lettered on the Deuce of Bells *Viel* and on the Deuce of Hearts *Glück.*
Woodcuts. Each 8.8 × 7.3 cm.
E.580.1-16—1885

191

Cards (23). 1750. [G.1058-1080; Bierdimpfle Nos.25 & 66]
Lettered on the Six of Hearts *C.K.S.Ambt.*, on the Deuce of Acorns *XX*, on the Deuce of Leaves *XXX/XXVI*, on the King of Acorns *B H* [*Burghausen*], on the King of Bells *L H* [*Landshut*], and on the King of Leaves *S.T.*
Woodcuts. Each 9.3 × 5.2 cm.
E.582.1-25—1885

192

Cards (18). 1753. [G.1081-1098; Bierdimpfle Nos.26 & 27; Keller, GER 199]
Lettered on the Deuce of Acorns *IIV/XXX/III*, and on the Kings of Leaves and Bells, as above.
Woodcuts. Each 9.5 × 5.7 cm.
E.583.1-18—1885

193

Cards (18). 1753. [G.1099-1116; Bierdimpfle Nos.28 & 69; Keller, GER 200]
Lettered on a strip of paper with name of publisher and date *1757*.
Lettered on the Six of Hearts *C.K.S.Ambt München*, on the Deuce of Acorns *XXXVIII*, and on the Kings of Acorns and Leaves, as above.
Woodcuts. Each 9.5 × 6 cm.
E.585.1-19—1885

194

Cards (18). As above, but the block badly damaged. [G.1188-1205; Bierdimpfle Nos.27 & 68; Keller, GER 198]
Lettered on the Deuce of Acorns *XXVI/ IIIIIXIVI*, and on the Kings of Acorns and Leaves, as above.
Woodcuts. Each 9.7 × 5.8 cm.
E.584.1-18—1885

195

Cards (18). Post 1764. [Bierdimpfle No.30; Keller, GER 196]
Lettered on the Deuce of Acorns *XXXVIII*, and on the Deuce of Hearts *CKSAM*.
Lettered on the Kings of Acorns, Bells and Leaves, as above.
Woodcuts. Each 9.4 × 5.9 cm.
E.587.1-18—1885

196

Cards (18). As above. [?G.1170-1187; Bierdimpfle Nos.29 & 70; Keller, GER 197]
Lettered on the Deuce of Acorns *XXXVIII*, and on the Six of Hearts *C.K.S. Ambt München*. Lettered on the Kings of Acorns, Bells and Leaves, as above.
Woodcuts. Each 9.6 × 5.5 cm.
E.586.1-18—1885

Keller, dates the cards c.1770. Though the lettering is identical, this pack is not identical in design to E.585—1885.

197

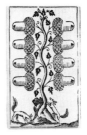

Cards (18). Similar but with a variant design to the above packs. The Kings bear cruder devices within the shields and are of a variant design, facing to left instead of to right. [Bierdimpfle Nos.31 & 72; Keller, GER 191]
Lettered on the Deuce of Acorns *XX/ I.III:/IVIIX*.
Woodcuts. Each 9.6 × 5.8 cm.
E.589.1-18—1885

Keller, dates the cards to the mid 18th century.

198

Cards (17), the numerals have in some cases little figures of men and women selling various wares, a dog and a pig on the Ten of Bells, two foxes on the Eight of Leaves, etc. [Bierdimpfle No.30]
Lettered on the Ten of Bells *X*.
Woodcuts. Each 9.4 × 5.6 cm.
E.588.1-17—1885

199

Tarot cards (38), the atouts, except the first and the last, with natural history subjects. The first with a harlequin and the last with a man balancing a hat on a stick on the end of his nose. The courts are full length figures, the Kings are on horseback. Published by the Churfürstl. Sigl-Amt., Munich, c.1770. [Bierdimpfle No.53]
Lettered on the Knave *CKSAM*. The atouts (except the last) with Roman numerals.
Woodcuts. Each 11.4 × 5.8 cm.
E.590.1-38—1885

200

Pack of 36 geographical cards describing the various divisions of Bavaria.
Backs with diaper star pattern. [Bierdimpfle, No.35]
With letterpress descriptions, dates etc.
Woodcuts, coloured by hand. Each 10.4 × 6.4 cm.
E.6305.1-36—1910 (no.1341—1872)

201

Würst (Sausage). Card from a pack of 32 in a game entitled 'Hexespiel' (Witches game) or 'Vogelspiel' (Bird game). Bavarian, early 19th century.
Lettered *Würst*.
Woodcut, coloured by hand. 8.8 × 5.9 cm.
E.6310—1910 (no.1346—1872)

The game originated in Italy where it is called the 'Cuckoo' game.

GREEK

202

Pack of 52 cards, the suit signs Italian, double-ended, the courts show ancient heroes. Published by the 'Hope' playing card makers, Corfu, late 19th century. Backs with a classical vase of flowers on a pedestal.
Lettered in Greek on the Ace of Money with name of makers etc and on the remaining Aces with more lettering.
Colour lithographs. Each 9.5 × 4.8 cm (CR)
E.23217.1-52—1957
Given by Mrs Amelia Logothetis

ITALIAN

203

Tarot cards (4): Stella, the Knave of Money, Death, wearing a cardinal's hat and mantellata, and the Ace of Cups, showing a fountain inscribed *nec spe nec metu*, with a cupid on either side, one of whom holds a shield with the arms of Colleoni. [Dummett, p.72 (12), pl.8; B.N.4, pl.22]
Watercolour, varnished, on illuminated background with diaper pattern.
Each 17 × 8.5 cm.
E.1468-1471—1926
Croft Lyons Bequest

These cards are formerly attributed to Antonio di Cicognara: see the introduction.

204

Minichiate Istoriche. Pack of minichiate cards (96, the Matto missing): the four suits each of 14 cards, lettered with historical details of Persia (Cups), Rome (Batons), Greece (Swords) and Assyria (Money) and the 40 atouts, numbered throughout, illustrating biblical, historical and mythological events etc. Backs decorated with a figure emblematic of 'History' seated among the ruins of Rome and lettered *Testis Temporum*. Florence, 1725. [Hoffmann, pl.69b]

Stamped on the atout XXXII with the stamp of an unidentified collector and inscribed in ink *Anton Pius Molinelli* (the rest illegible). See also E.822—1939.

205

Engravings, printed in red and black, with woodcuts pasted on the backs and overlapping to form a border round the card face. Each 10 × 5.9 cm.
E.822,1-96—1939
Given by Mr Robert Cust

206

Cards (24) from an incomplete pack, in 5 sheets before cutting. First half of 18th century.
Lettered *In Ascoli carte fine*.
Engravings. Size of sheets E.135 9.5 × 19.7 cm.; E.136-139 9.5 × 25.3 cm.
E.135-139—1944

207

Pack of 97 Florentine minichiate cards. Late 18th century.
Backs with the arms of the Medici.
[Hoffmann, pl. 69b; O'Donoghue, 47; Keller, ITA 55]
Stamped on the atout XXX with the stamp of an unidentified collector and inscribed in ink *Anton Pius Molinelli*. See also E.822—1939.
Engravings, with woodcuts pasted on the backs and overlapping to form a border round the card face. Each 10 × 5.7 cm.
E.527.1-97—1890

208

? The Knave of Diamonds. Card with French suit sign, full length figure, left profile. Back plain. ?Early 19th century. Used as a visiting card. Inscribed on the back *Künhaus Segreto: di S.E.Residte d'Inghilterra*.
Woodcut and colour stencil.
E.916—1933

209

Cards (4), French suit signs, backs plain.
? Italian, early 19th century.
Used as visiting cards.
Inscribed variously in French and in
Italian.
Stencil. Various sizes.
E.917-921—1933

JAPANESE

210

The Poem Game (Tuta garuta). Pack of
200 cards. 100 of the cards represent
each a poet, with the first half of a poem;
the remaining cards bear the conclusions
of the poems. In two black lacquer cases
contained in a black lacquer box.
Watercolour. Each 9 × 6 cm.
E.1024,1025—1928
Given by Mrs Gabrielle Enthoven

RUSSIAN, late 19th century

211

Pack of 36 trappola cards, German
suited, sometimes known as the 'Circus'
pack, from the figures on the suit of
Leaves. Backs decorated with a trellis
and quatrefoil pattern in red. [Hargrave,
p.276, 277] With fragmentary red
wrapper.
Stamped on the Deuce of Bells with the
duty stamp of the Foundling Hospital
(*Imperatorskago Vospitatel'Nago Doma*).
Colour lithographs. Each 9.6 × 5.9 cm.
E.1847.1-36—1885

212

Packs (2) of 52 cards each, standard,
French suited, courts double-ended.
Backs decorated with trailing stems.
With fragmentary yellow wrapper.
Colour lithographs. Each 8.9 × 5.7 cm.
E.1864.1-52—1885
E.1843.1-52—1885
E.1846.1-32—1885 (incomplete pack)

Backs as in E.1833—1885, but in red
and blue respectively.

213

Packs (3) of 52 cards each, as above, with
variant details, e.g. the Knave of Spades
has axe with suit sign and broken
outline. Backs decorated with diagonal
undulating stems in red (2) and in blue
respectively. One red, one blue, one
brown wrapper. No Monopoly Seals or
Duty Stamps on the packs
E.1841,1842—1885.
E.1844 stamped on the three of
Diamonds with Foundling Hospital
Duty stamp.
E.1841,1842,1844—1885

214

Another pack with variant details in the
court cards, e.g. the Knave of Spades is
without the suit sign in the axe. Backs
decorated with parallel lines of dots and
horizontal S shapes in blue. With
fragmentary pink wrapper.
Colour lithographs. Each 8.5 × 5.7 cm.
E.1833.1-52—1885

215

Identical pack, but with backs decorated
with undulating stems in blue (see
E.1841,1842—1885), and with blue
wrapper.
E.1870.1-52—1885

216

Another pack with variant details in the court cards, e.g. the Knave of Spades is without the suit sign in the axe (but the figure not identical to E.1833 and 1870—1885). Backs decorated with trailing stems in red (same as E.1864—1885). Fragmentary yellow wrapper. Stamped on the Ace of Diamonds with Foundling Hospital Duty stamp.
Colour lithographs. Each 8.9 × 5.7 cm.
E.1835.1-52—1885

217

Packs (2) of 52 cards each, courts double-ended, with figures in armour or in 16th century costume. Back decorated with arabesque interlacing pattern (as E.1845—1885). E.1866 with yellow wrapper, and back decorated with red diagonal plaid pattern.
The Ace of Diamonds bears the Monopoly Seal incorporating the stamp of the Foundling Hospital.
Colour lithographs. Each 8.9 × 5.7 cm.
E.1850.1-52,1866.1-52—1885

218

Two other packs, backs decorated with blue plaid pattern and yellow and red plaid pattern, respectively. With blue, and yellow wrappers.
E.1854.1-52,1866.1-52—1885

219

Pack of 52 cards, non-standard, double-ended courts, King of Hearts holds the suit sign in a drinking vessel, the Queen holds the suit sign in her hand, and the Knave is a Harlequin. The Queen of Clubs plays a harp, the Knave is a Scribe. The Knave of Diamonds blows a trumpet, and the Knave of Spades leans with clasped hands on an axe head.
The Ace of Diamonds bears the Monopoly Seal incorporating the Foundling Hospital Duty stamp.
Lettered on the King of Spades in Russian *Sciences Arts*. [Tilley, p.88, pl.56]
Colour lithographs. Each 6.9 × 4.8 cm.
E.1863.1-52—1885

Backs are decorated with a gold star trellis (as E.1871.1-52—1885)
With pictorial wrapper showing a coaching scene.

220

Another pack, identical, but with backs decorated with gold and pink star trellis.
E.1848.1-52—1885

221

Pack of 52 cards, double-ended. Backs decorated with stem sprays. With green wrapper. [Keller, RUS 2]
The Ace of Diamonds bears the Seal of Monopoly incorporating the Foundling Hospital Duty stamp.
Colour lithographs. Each 8.9 × 5.7 cm.
E.1853.1-52—1885

222

Similar pack, backs decorated with diagonal zig-zag club pattern (as E.1838,1-52—1885)
E.1855.1-52—1885

223

Packs (2) of 52 cards each, standard, courts double-ended, Knave of Spades with axe in left hand, blade facing edge of card. Back decorated with stem and leaf pattern in red (as E.1852—1885), and with diagonal zig-zag and club motif in blue (as E.1855—1885). With fragmentary turquoise and green wrappers respectively.
The Ace of Diamonds bears the Seal of Monopoly incorporating the Foundling Hospital Duty stamp.
Colour lithographs. Each 8.9 × 5.7 cm.
E.1838,1-52,1839.1-52—1885

224

Another pack, with slight variations from above, and with Ace of Diamonds bearing the Seal of Monopoly incorporating the Foundling Hospital Duty stamp in gold. Backs decorated with arabesque interlacing pattern (as E.1845,1850—1885). With pictorial wrapper printed in brown.
E.1845.1-52—1885

225

Packs (2) each of 52 cards; courts which are double-ended represent Egyptian, Chinese, African and Russian figures; the Aces, a ship, a leopard, a lion and an eagle respectively. Backs decorated with a star trellis in red and blue respectively. In slip-case with lettering in Russian, and with fragmentary wrapper.
Colour lithographs. Each 6.1 × 4.4 cm.; in case 6.9 × 4.8 cm.
E.1871.1-52,1872.1-52—1885

SPANISH

226

Miniature packs (2), standard suits. Backs with trellis and star pattern, red and blue, respectively, c.1870.
Colour lithographs. Each 4.9 × 3.6 cm.
nos. 29437, 29438,1-48

227

Cards (24, from a pack of 48), the Deuce to Nine of Batons, Cups and Money missing. 3rd quarter of 19th century. Backs plain. Reprints. [Bierdimpfle No.11]
Woodcuts. Each 9.2 × 6 cm.
E.578.1-24—1885

228

The Three of Money. Spanish, ? mid-19th century. Backs with large leaf pattern in blue.
Lithograph and colour stencil. 9.2 × 6.1 cm.
no.14098

229

The two of Cups. Back with diaper arrow pattern. Early 19th century. Woodcut and colour stencil. 8.3 × 5.4 cm.
no.13186

SWISS

230

Uncut sheet of 42 cards, arranged in seven vertical rows of six cards each. Basle, c.1500. [Schreiber, pl.VII] Woodcut. Size of sheet 40.6 × 26 cm.
E.10—1942

231

Cards (2), the Deuce of Shields and the Knave of Shields. ? late 17th century. Backs with cross within octagon pattern. Woodcuts and colour stencil. Each 6 × 3.6 cm.
E.4614, 4615—1907

This back pattern appears on German cards as early as the 16th century.

THAILAND

232

Packs (5), each of 30 cards, consisting of three suits (Birds, Men and Eyes) each of nine cards and one master card (the Lord, the Lady and the Gentleman respectively). 20th century.
E.1948A.1-30 inscribed on the backs with number, name of suit to which each card belongs. E.1948 D.1-30 mounted on cardboard and inscribed with a key to the sequence and numbering of each suit.
Colour lithographs. Each 7.6 × 2.2 cm (CR)
E.1948,1948A-D—1952
Given by Col. Amnuay Chya-Rochana

Four of these packs are used to play the game known as 'Pai Tong'.

233

Plates (9) from *A Pack of Cavalier Playing Cards*, published by Edmund Goldschmid, for the Aungervyle and Clarendon Historical Societies, Edinburgh, 1885. Each plate contains four cards, numerals V to X, and courts of each suit. With letterpress notice sheet.
Engravings. Size of sheets, each 22 × 15 cm.
E.1498-1506—1899

Goldschmid was honorary secretary of the Aungervyle and Clarendon Societies, who at the same time issued a facsimile pack of 52 cards (see below).

234

Pack of 52 cards, reproductions of a pack known as 'The Rump Parliament' or 'A complete political satire of The Commonwealth', possibly made in Holland during Charles II's exile. Published by Edmund Goldschmid, Edinburgh, 1885. [Morley, pp.174,175; Hargrave, p.192; Willshire, E.195; S.Mann, pp.151,152; Keller, ENG 99; J.Berry, No.239]
With a lid of original box labelled in letterpress *A Pack of Cavalier Playing Cards Temp. Charles II. Forming A Complete Political Satire of The Commonwealth The Original Pack, of which this is a Facsimile, is in the possession of the Right Hon. Earl Nelson,* etc.
The label inscribed in ink with copyright date *16.8.86*.
Lithographs. Each 9.8 × 6.2 cm.
E.62-113—1911

Only three perfect packs are known to exist, one of which has an additional card lettered 'To be sold by R.T. near Stationer Hall, at the Black Bull in Cornhill'.

235

Sheet of cards (16, from a pack of 46) by Hans Sebald Beham (1500—1550). [Hoffmann, pl.42b]. Lippmann reproduction.
E.2926—1934

236

G Pauli *Hans Sebald Beham*, Strasbourg, 1901, No.1464: the attribution to Beham is refuted by Pauli.

BIBLIOGRAPHY

Clarkson, Tom, *Tarot the Life-Enhancer*, Woking, 1983

D'Allemagne, H R D, *Les Cartes à Jouer*, Paris, 1906

De La Rue Journal, Festival Number, 13 July 1951

De Vesme, A, & Dearborn Massar, P D, *Stefano Della Bella*, New York, 1971

Die Cotta'schen Spielkarten Almanache 1805–1811, catalogue of the exhibition held at the Deutsches Spielkarten Museum, Bielefeld, 1968–69

Dummett, Michael, *The Game of Tarot*, London, Duckworth, 1980

Grupp, C D, *Spielkarten und ihre Geschichte*, Leinfelden, 1973

Hicklin, F, *Playing Cards*, London, HMSO, 1976 (out of print)

Hochman, Gene, *Encyclopaedia of American Playing Cards*, 1977

Hutton, Alice, *The Cards Can't Lie*, London, 1979

Mann, Sylvia, *Collecting Playing Cards*, Worcester & London, 1966

O'Dell-Franke, Ilse, *Kupferstiche und Radierungen aus der Werkstatt des Virgil Solis*, Wiesbaden, 1977

Ottley W Y, *A Collection of Fac-Similes of Scarce and Curious Prints*, London, 1828

Pauli, G, *Hans Sebald Beham*, Strasbourg, 1901

Séguin, J, *Le Jeu de Carte*, Paris, 1968

Tilley, R, *Playing Cards*, London, Weidenfeld & Nicolson, 1967

CATALOGUES RAISONNÉES

Titles are listed under the abbreviations that appear in the catalogue.

Bierdimpfle Bierdimpfle, K A, *Die Sammlung der Spielkarten des Baierischen Nationalmuseums*, Munich, 1884

B N *Tarot, Jeu et Magie*, catalogue of the exhibition held at the Bibliothèque Nationale, Paris, 1884–85

D H & M D Hoffmann, D and Dietrich, M, *Die Dondorfschen Luxus-Spielkarten*, Harenberg, 1981

François François, A, *Histoire de la Carte à Jouer*, Paris, 1974

G M *Katalog der in germanischen Museum befindlichen Kartenspiele und Spielkarten*, Nuremberg, 1886

Hargrave Hargrave, C P, *A History of Playing Cards and a Bibliography of Cards and Gaming*, Boston & New York, 1930

Hoffmann Hoffmann, D, *Die Welt der Spielkarte Eine Kulturgeschichte*, Munich, 1972

Hoffmann F Hoffmann, D, *Spielkarten des Historiches Museums Frankfurt-am-Main*, Frankfurt-am-Main, 1972

Kaplan Kaplan, S R, *The Encyclopaedia of Tarot*, New York, 1978

Keller Keller, W, *A Catalogue of the Cary Collection of Playing Cards in the Yale University Library*, Vols I-IV, New Haven, Yale University Library, 1981

Lehrs Lehrs, Max, *Geschichte und Kritscher Katalog des Deutschen, Niederländischen und Französischen Kupferstichs im XV Jahrhundert*, Vienna, 1930

Mann Mann, S, *Collecting Playing Cards*, Worcester & London, 1966

Morley Morley, H T, *Old and Curious Playing Cards Their History and Types from many Countries and Periods*, London, 1931

O'Donoghue O'Donoghue, F M, *Catalogue of the Collection of Playing Cards bequeathed to the Trustees of the British Museum by the late Lady Charlotte Schreiber*, London, British Museum, 1901

Schreiber Schreiber, W L, *Die ältesten Spielkarten und die auf das Kartenspiel Bezug habenden Urkunden des 14. und 15. Jahrhunderts*, Strasbourg, 1937

Willshire Willshire, W H, *A Descriptive Catalogue of Playing and Other Cards in the British Museum accompanied by a Concise General History of the Subject and Remarks on Cards of Divination and of a Politico-Historical Character*, London, British Museum, 1876

INDEX

In this index, references to page numbers are in roman
and references to catalogue numbers are in **bold**.

Printed in the United Kingdom for Her Majesty's Stationery Office
Dd 289358 C50 10/88